M000200858

The Taxable
Investor's Manifesto

Also by Stuart Lucas

Wealth: Grow It, Protect It, Spend It and Share It

Wealth: Grow It and Protect It

The Taxable Investor's Manifesto

Wealth Management Strategies to Last a Lifetime

Stuart E. Lucas

WILEY

For general information on our other products and services or for technical support, please contact our Customer Care Department within the United States at (800) 762-2974, outside the United States at (317) 572-3993 or fax (317) 572-4002.

Wiley publishes in a variety of print and electronic formats and by print-on-demand. Some material included with standard print versions of this book may not be included in e-books or in print-on-demand. If this book refers to media such as a CD or DVD that is not included in the version you purchased, you may download this material at http://booksupport.wiley .com. For more information about Wiley products, visit www.wiley.com.

Library of Congress Cataloging-in-Publication Data
Names: Lucas, Stuart E., author.
Title: The taxable investor's manifesto : wealth management strategies to
    last a lifetime / Stuart E. Lucas.
Description: Hoboken, New Jersey : Wiley, [2020] | Includes index.
Identifiers: LCCN 2020004855 (print) | LCCN 2020004856 (ebook) | ISBN
    9781119692034 (hardback) | ISBN 9781119691990 (ePDF) | ISBN
    9781119692027 (epub)
Subjects: LCSH: Investments. | Finance, Personal. | Stocks. | Portfolio
    management. | Investments—Taxation.
Classification: LCC HG4521 .L86155 2020 (print) | LCC HG4521 (ebook) |
    DDC 332.6—dc23
LC record available at https://lccn.loc.gov/2020004855
LC ebook record available at https://lccn.loc.gov/2020004856

Cover Design: Wiley
Cover Image: © sorbetto/Getty Images modified by Wiley

Printed in the United States of America

10 9 8 7 6 5 4 3 2 1

To Becca, Camilla, and Sam

Author's Legal Information, Disclaimer, and Disclosure

The author, through his firm, Wealth Strategist Partners, LLC provides investment advice and functions as an outsourced Chief Investment Officer for taxable individuals and families. Any statements or information contained in this book are made in the author's personal capacity and are not affiliated with, or endorsed by, any investment adviser with which the author may currently, or in the future will, be associated.

The information and views contained in this material are as of the dates noted and are for educational and informational purposes only. Such views are subject to change without notice. Neither Mr. Lucas nor Wealth Strategist Partners have any duty or obligation to update the information in this book. The information presented does not constitute, and should not be construed as, investment advice or recommendations with respect to markets, asset allocation, funds, securities, or individual investments. Moreover, neither the information nor any opinions expressed constitutes a solicitation for the purchase or sale of any investment or security.

Readers should consider their personal circumstances and consult with their own qualified investment, tax, and legal advisors. Neither the author, nor Wealth Strategist Partners, LLC, nor the publisher can be held responsible for any losses or damages arising from any use of this information.

Certain information contained herein is based on independent third-party sources. The author believes that the sources from which such information has been obtained are reliable; however, he cannot ensure the information's accuracy and it has not independently been verified for accuracy, completeness, or the veracity of assumptions used.

Investment performance information should not be relied upon as the primary reason for making investment decisions. Historical investment performance is not a reliable predictor of future performance. The potential for profit also creates the possibility of loss. Tax rates change regularly, and such changes may have a material impact on the expressed views herein and the attractiveness of certain investments.

MORNINGSTAR, INC. DISCLAIMER

Contents

About the Author

Stuart E. Lucas is founder, Co-Managing Partner, and Chief Investment Officer of Wealth Strategist Partners, advisor to large complex families across financial, business, and cultural dimensions of their enterprises.

Stuart designed and is Co-Director of the University of Chicago Booth School of Business's Private Wealth Management continuing education program, which has served over 1,000 wealthy individuals and families in the 12 years since the course's inception. He is a speaker on topics of wealth management around the world. His first book, *Wealth: Grow It and Protect It* (FT Press), has been published on three continents. He is the author of numerous articles on investing and wealth management, most recently "The 50% Rule" and "Pick Your Battles" (*Journal of Wealth Management*), co-authored with Alejandro Sanz.

Stuart is chairman of the Investment Committee of National Public Radio in Washington, D.C., and is involved in various other philanthropic endeavors in education and media.

Previously, Stuart was the senior managing director of the Ultra-High Net Worth Group within Private Client Services at Bank One (now JP Morgan Chase); director of a multifamily investment office in Paris, France; general manager of European operations of Wellington Management Company in London, England; and assistant portfolio manager of a Forbes Honor Roll mutual fund.

He has a BA with honors from Dartmouth College, an MBA from Harvard Business School, and is a Chartered Financial Analyst. He has been married for more than 30 years to his wife, Susan, and they have three grown children.

Acknowledgments

Over the years, in my day job, in academia, in my role as chair of National Public Radio's Investment Committee, I am blessed to have built relationships, some spanning 40 years, with brilliant, committed investors. So much of what I have learned about leadership, about investing, about managing taxable wealth, is the result of shared inquiry and the desire to get better and better at our craft. As a result, my book has few ideas I can justifiably call my own. More powerfully, it is the product of that collective inquiry. Possibly the most original idea is simply to weave the insights of others into a hopefully coherent whole.

My journey started as a newly minted Dartmouth history major and aspiring equity analyst at Wellington Management Company. My experience at Wellington and three years of preparation to earn the CFA Charter holder designation gave me the conceptual frameworks to do my job well and defined the rigor with which I have approached my career ever since. The ethical precepts and the professional networks exemplified by both organizations are foundations of my investment worldview for which I am eternally grateful.

Those underpinnings and the relationships that developed with them led to over two dozen busy investment professionals, including Seth Masters, Rick Roeding, Bill Poorvu, Howard Marks, David Puth, Trent Sebits, Shirley Spence, David Jones, Gena Estenfelder Todd, Howard Stevenson, and others, graciously taking the time to read and provide detailed feedback on versions of this manifesto, some of you more than once. The value of your wise insights and honest feedback is priceless and the book's content and readability are infinitely improved as a result. I look forward to continuing our thought partnership in the years ahead.

I have a special group of thought partners that deserve acknowledgment too: my fellow faculty members in the University of Chicago's Private Wealth Management Program. We are now in our thirteenth year and John Heaton, Steven Kaplan, Sara Hamilton, and Howard Helsinger have co-taught every single program with me. I have learned a great deal from you, and a lot of that wisdom has found its way into the book. Steve has been a wise advisor on private equity and venture capital, as well as a personal mentor and advocate. Chapter 5 of this book would not have been written if John Heaton hadn't sensitized me to the power and the math of time horizons. I'd been a long-term investor for decades and understood intuitively the effects of horizon on risk, but John provided the gateway to the statistical analysis. Howard Helsinger's way of teaching estate planning, integrating highly nuanced legal strategies in an envelope of human values and empathy, is extremely impactful. Sara brings to PWM more than 30 years of experience serving family offices through her firm, Family Office Exchange. In the very first PWM program in 2007, I was approached by José Ramón Sanz to develop a parallel curriculum in Spain. Ever since, we have had a wonderful intellectual and business partnership as well as a great friendship that has sprung from teaching and learning from wealthy Spanish-speaking families. It's from José Ramón that I became particularly sensitized to the issues, challenges, and opportunities of being a business-owning family over multiple generations.

Over the last two decades my clients at Wealth Strategist Partners have trusted me to implement the strategies that are revealed in this book. Of course, working with them, deliberating their insightful questions, managing with them through periods of stress and market volatility, helping them transition through liquidity events and from one generation to the next, have all been great opportunities for me to learn. Numerous private investors and family office executives have provided additional analysis and practical advice born of experience. The lens of learning what works through experience has no replacement; I am grateful for the partnerships that have made that experience possible.

My colleagues and business partners push me every day. To one degree or another you have all contributed to the ideas, the writing, and the editing of this book. You also were patient with me when I have been distracted by the enormity of this project. Thank you.

Thank you also to competitors and investment managers whom I've reached out to for help. You've given me valuable feedback and helped me to dig up relevant research, encouraging me along this path, and distributing the finished product to your colleagues, clients, and friends.

Thank you all for sharing the ride with me and contributing to the development of any wisdom that may appear in these pages. This book is as much yours as it is mine, but I will take responsibility for all the points you disagree with and for any factual mistakes. I hope I've done you proud.

I also wish to thank my editor, Bill Falloon, and Wiley, my publisher. They have been great partners and supporters of this project, providers of constructive feedback, and they moved expeditiously to bring this book to life.

Lastly, thank you to my family. My father and my late mother raised me right and helped me to flourish. My siblings and their spouses, especially Boutie and Melissa Lucas, are willing collaborators in our family enterprise. Some are engaged every day; the others hold us accountable in thoughtful, constructive ways. My children, nieces, and nephews are making their own way in the world, developing their own careers, and making their parents proud. This book would not exist without them being the people they are.

The best decision I ever made was to ask Susan to marry me thirty years ago. We are only just getting started. In addition to being the love of my life and my partner raising our three wonderful children, she has also been my business partner for ten years. A compassionate wonderful human being, she is also a highly gifted leader and businessperson. She supports me emotionally; she is a fantastic thought partner and an excellent editor. Her hands are all over this book. I truly am the luckiest guy in the world.

Introduction

This is not a book about tax; it's about fomenting a quiet revolution. *The Taxable Investor's Manifesto* is your guide to maximizing profit from your financial assets over a lifetime and beyond. It's also a book about how to compete side by side against the majority of investors who don't pay tax. And it's about the skilled advisors who will help you manage your hard-earned wealth most effectively.

Taxable investors need to think differently. It's my experience; it's my mantra. It's the truth. And yet, try to find comprehensive guidance about personal finance that makes a serious stab at optimizing the combined effects of the money we earn, our investments, and the taxes we pay. It's darn near impossible, and I know where to look. I have spent 35 years in the investment and wealth management industries and received thorough academic and professional training.

The bottom line is that almost everyone who studies finance academically or advises us about our personal finances treats taxes as an afterthought, at best. It's very difficult for academics to access the diffuse data they would need to study our after-tax investment returns, so they don't. As a result, financial advisors haven't received sufficient training to optimize the returns to their taxable clients. In addition, the metrics that academia and the financial industry have developed to assess performance are designed without consideration of tax impact. When proper metrics don't exist, firms don't have the tools to monitor and incentivize their advisors to reduce our tax bill, and we have a hard time understanding what we are missing. These omissions are all rational given the current circumstances. But they come at a large cost. If academics, advisors, training program designers, and taxable clients all pull together, we can change the wealth management industry for the better.

Why should we care? For starters, the right advice is worth a great deal of money; to the tune of $5 million on an initial $1 million investment. That's good for clients and it's good for the fee base on which advisors earn their living. Let me explain. Unbeknown to me, a sophisticated investor who read a draft of this manifesto modeled the likely after-tax profit over 30 years on a $1 million initial investment under two scenarios. First, he modeled his existing portfolio of cash, fixed income, hedge funds, and actively managed equities. Roughly 60% of the portfolio was in equities. Second, he modeled a portfolio using the manifesto's strategy. With the same assumptions for market returns and for tax rates, using his current strategy the portfolio grew to about $4 million over 30 years; using the manifesto's strategy, $9 million, after tax. I was shocked by the difference. I knew it would be big, but until then I hadn't done the math. So I hired an analyst to build his own model. The answer was similar. A $5 million difference; that's why investors should care and that's why their advisors should care. Their interests are aligned to maximize after-tax returns. By the way, whether you start with $100,000 or $10 million, or even a billion dollars, the benefits are proportional. Is that potential impact worth a few hours of your time? Make your own assumptions. Do your own math. You will see the difference.

What are the underlying sources of that huge difference, and why is the difference so much larger than if a tax-exempt investor employed the same model? Shifting to a more equity-heavy portfolio benefits both types of investor, because over the long run equities have outperformed bonds, cash, and most hedge funds. But for the taxable investor the impact is much more profound. Because of the nature of our tax system, most of the profits on fixed income and hedge funds are taxed each year, and they are taxed at higher rates. Managing equities in a tax-efficient way enables investors to defer the payment of taxes for years and years, sometimes decades. A properly structured investment portfolio reduces tax drag and dramatically increases the power of compounding.

The combination of equities, time, tax efficiency, and compounding can be worth millions.

Let me be clear. I firmly believe that it is the civic duty of every successful American to pay taxes; it's a responsibility and a privilege. Cognizant of the many benefits of living, working, and raising a family here, I am happy to pay my share. This manifesto simply advises that taxable investors should develop investment strategies with the tax and estate planning implications rigorously embedded in their design and management process. Doing so is common sense, if not commonly employed. Plus, it reinforces a healthy long-term perspective, a business-owning mindset, and, with a vibrant economy, a larger tax base.

For those of us who are trying to save for retirement and accumulate additional wealth through our careers, through employment income or by starting and growing businesses, the difference in asset accumulation, financial security, and lifestyle between average wealth management and good wealth management is huge. The manifesto's strategy becomes even more compelling when an investor is managing wealth multigenerationally. It is also a guide for navigating over much longer time frames and through a maze of estate and gift tax laws.

The quest to understand and manage taxable wealth is personal for me. My great-grandfather started the Carnation Company in 1899. After 86 years the company was sold and we shifted from being a business-owning family to a "financial family." I've been lucky: lucky to be born into wealth, lucky to get a great education, lucky to get superb training as a professional investor, lucky to teach. All these experiences, all the learning, are crystalized in this manifesto. My goal in writing it and sharing it is to change the world in one small way: together, with common knowledge and resonant voices we can find a better way to manage taxable financial assets, secure financial futures, and provide higher-quality advice.

My previous book, *Wealth: Grow It and Protect It,* was published in 2006. Its goal is to help wealth owners to manage their wealth strategically and comprehensively across business, financial, and cultural dimensions. It all starts from establishing a purpose for their wealth, based on their core values. More than twelve years and a second edition later, the book is still in print. People are still buying it, reading it, implementing it, thanking me for writing it, and coming to me for further advice. With some frequency, readers show me their copy with 30 separate pages or more dog-eared and highlighted. It's incredibly gratifying to be able to help people in this way. Hopefully, *The Taxable Investor's Manifesto* will have similar impact and similar longevity.

In *Wealth,* I offer eight principles of wealth management. The very first one is: Take Charge. Over the last 35 years as the wealth strategist on behalf of my clients – including my family – and myself, I've learned that no one is in better position to optimize your wealth than you.

In writing *The Taxable Investor's Manifesto,* I've drawn from a lot of sources: from the wisdom of others, from experience gained from making mistakes with my own money, and from careful analysis across investing, tax, and estate planning disciplines to figure out how to do it better. What I've learned applies to every taxable investor, regardless of how much wealth he or she has been fortunate to accumulate. After reading and studying you will understand why taxable investors and their advisors need to think and act differently, and you will learn how to do so. Integrating the combined effects of investing, tax management, and estate planning is good financial management and good business. Good financial management leads to effective wealth management; doing it right will help you grow your assets faster and with less effort.

Managing taxable wealth well can be powerfully simple: lower friction costs, raise return potential, and extend your time horizon (in the context of this book, friction costs are the combined drag of fees and taxes). Armed with a few key tools for success – clear objectives, aligned interests with your advisors, a decent system of accountability, and the discipline to persist with your game plan – your money will work for you, not the other way around. Then you can focus most of your attention on what really interests you and what you're really good at. A straightforward strategy is the right answer for most people who have full lives, are leading rewarding careers, and whose careers, families, and other callings are deserving of full attention. This integrated approach to taxable investing is a step-change in thinking that can help you build a more secure future and a more meaningful livelihood in an uncertain world. Nevertheless, because inertia is powerful and people don't change easily, unless you push for change and remain vigilant, change won't happen.

You can also make wealth management really complex. Complexity can add additional value, especially when managing on a multigenerational basis. But the hunt for superior investment returns – the place where most investors and most financial advisors focus their attention – is an extraordinarily competitive zero-sum game. You are competing against, or trying to align with, hundreds of thousands of well-trained professionals, most of whom extract high fees for uncertain value. Those who extract high fees have the resources and incentives to craft highly persuasive marketing efforts.[1] Is it their marketing or their skill that makes you think that by hiring them you will outperform? Can you tell the difference, especially after tax?

Adding to the challenge, good estate planning can create more value, more predictably, than investing. Good planning requires experienced, interdisciplinary talent and finely crafted strategy. Good estate planning also often leads to splitting assets into many small, legally distinct components and then needing to reassemble them to make the whole worth more than the sum of the parts. One friend calls it trying to put Humpty Dumpty back together again. Governance and administration become really complicated without good systems to manage all the disparate bits, individually and collectively. To pursue this complex path, it really helps to have large-scale, uncommon insight, shrewd hiring

---

[1] One of my favorite quotes from John "Jack" Bogle, the founder of Vanguard Group, comes from his April 13, 2004, "Gary M. Brinson Distinguished Lecture," where he speaks about why it was taking so long for indexing to catch on: "The problem faced by low cost no-load index funds is that ... almost all the darn money goes to the investor." For decades, index funds struggled to gain attention, in part because their "rents" were so low that the fund managers had few dollars to spend on marketing. Fourteen years later, in 2018, according to Morningstar, Inc., $301 billion flowed into index funds and $458 billion flowed out of active management. Investors are (finally) catching on and roughly $2 billion in annual "rent" charged by active managers evaporated.

practices, and strong discipline. You will need help; the right help is essential.

In this book, I explore both the straightforward and the more complex path. Fortunately, any family investment office, business owner, successful career builder, or young professional, regardless of the size of their wealth, can achieve success using either path. They simply need to match skill with strategy, build the right support structure, and follow the guideposts in this manifesto. Either path creates multiple ways to add value and does so with high odds of success; neither one embraces the traditional "holy grail" of "beating the market," upon which most wealth advisors market their wares.

For those readers who are interested, the manifesto cites academic and other well-researched literature to supply you with supporting data for key concepts. There is good research about taxable investing out there, but it is diffuse and hard to find. This manifesto aims to provide a single, comprehensive, accessible guide that taxable investors and their advisors can use to sharpen their own thinking, align interests, and improve results over decades, even generations, by millions of dollars.

The *Taxable Investor's Manifesto* is organized in a straightforward manner. Chapters 1 to 7 describe seven value drivers that pertain to everyone and that are straightforward to execute. They should be approached as a coordinated strategy, not something from which to cherry-pick one or two ideas. Each component adds value. Collectively, they are at their most powerful and profitable; if one component fails, you still have multiple ways to win. One can sum up this advice as a Hippocratic Oath for taxable investors: First, do no harm.

Chapters 8 and 9 describe opportunities for those with greater scale and the inclination for complexity to add incremental investment value net of taxes. In addition to considerable analytical skill, this requires excellent judgment about people and opportunity – judgment born of experience and independent thinking. Possibly the most difficult challenge here is allocating and reallocating capital effectively. As a taxable investor, every time you sell a successful investment you must share your gains with the government. Every time you pay tax, you are left with a smaller base of capital on which to compound returns going forward. If you're an advisor, every time your client pays investment-related taxes, those are assets on which you no longer earn fees. This complexity is not shared by tax-exempt investors or their advisors. It requires different perspective and special skill.

Chapters 10, 11, and 12 integrate the business, financial, and cultural elements of managing a complex, potentially multigenerational, family enterprise. At their core, family enterprises require values and vision that support a strong economic engine and a flourishing family. They also must navigate complex estate taxes and the evolution of control and ownership from one generation to the next. Building and managing all this in the face of change, uncertainty, and timeframes that can approach 50 years or more is no small challenge, but it can be done, and the results are powerful.

Chapter 13 is a reminder to everyone that investing involves risk. I explore the key risks to investing in this way, at least the ones I can foresee. It's important to process the risks to be alert to them and to not be distracted by the inevitable ups and downs of market movements that are unavoidable parts of the landscape.

Many wealth owners reading this manifesto are mulling over whether to manage their financial assets themselves or to hire an advisor to help them. Having read it, I believe that most will be convinced that choosing a skilled advisor is instrumental to long-term success. You will also have increasing conviction to identify the right advisor, hold them accountable, and compensate them appropriately. The right talent comes at a price but pays for itself many times over. In Chapter 14, I discuss how to choose the advisor you need to help you accomplish your objectives. The answer varies depending on your scale, the complexity of your circumstances, and your time horizon. The challenge is to find a person or team who offers what you need, has the mindset and skills to deliver on their promise, and whose interests are aligned with yours.

A word about financial advisors: many find themselves in a bind. Why? They know how difficult it is to beat the market, but they also know clients will pay them for advice that feels complicated even if it's unlikely to work. Even when advisors know that clients will get better results with a more straightforward solution, they fear that clients won't pay for what sounds simple and straightforward. The thinking goes that indexing is cheap and doesn't add value, so why pay an advisor to recommend it?

This manifesto illuminates a path out of this bind, to the benefit of both wealth owners and their advisors. There is so much value creation that goes into comprehensive, strategic, after-tax wealth management that has largely gone unrecognized, undelivered, unmeasured, and unpaid for. Looking forward, we can change this. Taxable investors deserve to get good advice and advisors deserve to get paid fairly for delivering it.

The Taxable
Investor's Manifesto

CHAPTER ONE

Taxable Investors Need to Think Differently

What makes a good investment? It's such a simple question, but not an easy one to answer. We never know in advance whether an investment will succeed. By their very nature, investments involve uncertainty. Nevertheless, one can evaluate proactively whether something is a good investment. To me, a good investment has more upside potential than downside risk; it's **asymmetric**. The investment becomes even more attractive when its upside can compound for a long time; it has high potential **magnitude**. A third valuable attribute is a favorable **probability of success**; 30% odds of doubling one's money is a lot better than 10% odds of doing so.

Another important characteristic that drives investment attractiveness is the percentage of the profit from a successful investment that the investor actually keeps, **profit retention**. Profit retention is different than asymmetry, magnitude, and probabilities because taxable and tax-exempt investors operate with different rules. A tax-exempt investor – like an endowment, foundation, or retirement plan – may keep 90% or more of the

1

profits from a high-yield bond fund each year, and it can reinvest the entire 90%. The other 10% or so goes to the fund manager in the form of fees. On the other hand, a taxable investor based in California or New York earns and can reinvest maybe 50% of the profits because, in addition to paying the investment manager, the taxable investor must also pay taxes on income and capital gains. Through the lens of that taxable investor, the management fees aren't 10% of retained profits; they are more like 20% of the after-tax return. It's the same investment but with very different results. For hedge funds the tax-exempt investor keeps maybe 75% because of the higher fee structure. On the same investment, the taxable investor nets 45% or less.[1]

Retaining 75% to 90% of the same gross profits versus 45% to 50% can have profound effects on symmetry, magnitude, and probability assessments, especially when asset growth compounds over years and decades. But almost no one – academics, advisors, clients – has done the math, measured the differences, and adapted investment strategy or tactics to take these differences into account.

When we pay tax, that portion of profit goes to the government and is no longer in our portfolio. It can't grow for us, it can't pay dividends, it's removed from an advisor's assets under management. On the other hand, if tax payments on an investment can be deferred, the amount that otherwise would be used to pay tax in a given year has the potential to keep compounding, indefinitely.

Success as taxable investors comes with additional challenges. The more we defer tax payments and the higher the magnitude of the gain, the bigger the tax bill at the eventual sale. A highly appreciated asset worth $1 million and paying a 2% dividend before tax could, after it is sold, end up being worth only $750,000 after capital gains taxes are paid. Over time, any replacement investment needs to appreciate at a faster rate than the old one just to break even in dollar terms, and it needs to generate a 33% dividend boost

---

[1] For a detailed analysis of the after-fee and after-tax returns of index funds, mutual funds, hedge funds, and private equity funds review, see Stuart Lucas and Alejandro Sanz, "The 50% Rule: Keep More Profit in Your Wallet," *Journal of Wealth Management* 20 (no.2, Fall 2017).

to maintain cash flow. This isn't an issue for tax-exempt investors, and their investment managers have no need to think through the problem.

Being seen as a successful money manager is good business. Skillfully crafted brochures and sales pitches describe investment processes that involve careful analysis of investment options, how decisions are made to buy the best ones, regular reevaluation of those decisions as relative values change, and how to upgrade the portfolio to achieve the best possible results. Tax-exempt investors are indifferent about whether a manager makes a thousand decisions a minute, ten a week, five a month, two a year, or none at all, as long as the results are there.

That's not the case for taxable investors. Through our lens there is a fundamental tension between manager activity and our net results. The combination of rising stock prices and manager activity can be very expensive for us, even when it benefits tax-exempt investors. Selling a financial asset triggers tax on profits; that tax reduces return, undermining profit retention and magnitude. None of it is reflected in the way investment performance is typically presented.[2]

Given all these differences, it's not acceptable to manage taxable and tax-exempt portfolios using the same investment theories, the same analysis, the same structures, and the same metrics of performance. We taxable investors need to think and act differently, and our advisors should too. This manifesto will tell you how.

We need to think differently because taxes claim between roughly a quarter to a half of potential profits, and taxes skew relative risk symmetry, profit magnitude, retention rate, and probabilities of winning. Plus, we aren't talking about just one investment. Most of us will make many investment decisions over decades and decades. We need to factor in the relationship of each investment to our entire investment program. Each time we

---

[2]This isn't entirely true. In their prospectuses – but rarely transferred into their marketing material – mutual funds are required to provide estimates of after-tax performance. This level of reporting is not required, and rarely calculated by Exchange Traded Funds, alternative investments like hedge funds and private equity funds, or separately managed accounts. But even for mutual funds this information is not widely circulated or analyzed.

receive interest income or dividends, we have to pay tax. Selling any investment also has tax consequences.

Importantly, the tax code tells us to sum all our investment gains and losses for a given year and pay tax only on the net realized gains over the course of that calendar year. If we have net realized investment losses in a year, they are "carried forward" to be offset against net realized gains in future years. Investment losses cannot be used in any material way to offset earned income for tax purposes[3] or to "claw back" previous taxes paid. It's an oversimplification, but think of tax on investments and on earned income as two separate, independent calculations.

Tax rates are not uniformly applied either: we pay a tax rate on investment income, on short-term capital gains, and on earned income that is about 50% higher than the rate payable on long-term capital gains. Unrealized capital gains can grow tax deferred until the security is sold, sometimes years or decades after purchase. But taxes on earnings, investment income, and realized gains must be paid currently. The character, scale, and timing of profits all impact what ends up in our pockets. When tax is paid, the opportunity to compound those lost dollars in our portfolio evaporates – forever.

In the world of taxable investors, the interplay of fees and taxes also affects profits. Depending on an investment's structure, sometimes fees reduce taxable and actual profits equally. For example, management fees and expenses in mutual funds and ETFs are deductible from profits before calculating taxes. However, under the Tax Cut and Jobs Act of 2017, for hedge funds, private equity funds, other limited partnership funds, and separate accounts, investment management fees do not reduce your taxable profits, even though they reduce your actual profits. You read this correctly, the investment structure causes taxable profits to be higher than actual profit. The tax character of these fees makes them particularly costly.

When these costs cannot be deducted from taxable profits, effective tax rates can soar, especially when pre-fee profits are

---

[3]Individuals may only deduct a maximum of $3,000 of final net short-term or long-term investment losses against other types of income.

modest. Let's take a simplified, but directionally correct, example. A taxpayer invests $100 with a hedge fund that earns a modest 4% return in a given year before management fees of 1.5% on invested capital, for a net return of 2.5%. The combination of factors – including characterization of income and the investor's state tax rate – result in a 35% tax rate applied to the investor's $4 gross, pre-fee profit. The resulting tax is $1.40. As a result, the investor pays an effective tax rate of 56% on $2.50 of after-fee, pretax profit, and is left with a measly $1.10 net, or 27.5% of the gross profit. As taxable investors, we need to evaluate the interplay among investments, taxes, and structures because it matters – a lot.

Figure 1.1 shows a straightforward framework for taxable investing.

Just because tax efficiency is valuable, it does not stand to reason that all tax-efficient investments are good. Life insurance is widely sold as a way to eliminate taxes on profits and to avoid estate taxes, but it will only be a good investment if the underlying structure, terms, and assets are sound. Similarly, Qualified Opportunity Zone funds, approved in the 2017 Tax Act, are tax efficient. But they will only serve taxable investors well if the underlying investments generate decent profits. One of the potential issues with vehicles that shield you from taxes is that if the investment turns out to be a loser, you will suffer 100%

FIGURE 1.1 A FRAMEWORK FOR TAXABLE INVESTING.

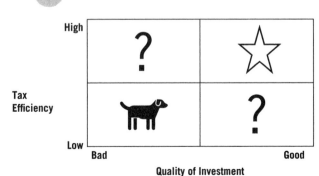

of the loss. Ironically, not all losses are bad if they are structured properly and the government is your partner in the loss. Later in the book, we will explore an investment technique called tax-loss harvesting, where one explicit purpose of the strategy is to realize losses in part of your investment portfolio to offset the tax otherwise payable on other realized investment profits.

Parenthetically, as we've already explored, some investments may appear to generate decent returns, but after being subjected to inefficient structures, high fees, and tax rates of 50% or more, in fact they aren't so great. As a general rule, the shorter the hold period of an investment and the more of its total return that comes in the form of taxable income, the higher the risk-adjusted, pretax returns need to be in order to justify their inclusion in taxable portfolios. In the chapters ahead, we will explore further how to invest in that upper-right-hand quadrant with consistency and success.

Most predictably, the best investments for taxable investors are ones that generate decent to strong capital gains for long periods of time. Nevertheless, even with success there are consequences. As unrealized gains grow, a rigidity creeps into taxable portfolios: the more successful an investment becomes, the more expensive it is to sell and the harder it is to replace. With greater rigidity, each decision about whether or not to sell becomes more important and more deserving of studied, professional analysis.

Estate planning can also have a big influence on where an investment falls in the two-by-two matrix shown in Figure 1.1. Anyone can establish tax-deferred or tax-exempt retirement plans. Assets that would otherwise be in the bottom half of the matrix move to the top half if they are in one of these vehicles. Tax-inefficient assets within retirement plans add diversification in the traditional sense. They also give you the means to manage future changes in tax rates. As wealth grows there is also the opportunity to share it with others: children, grandchildren, philanthropies. Good estate planning can be incredibly valuable, both for tax planning and for perpetuating family business.

In some ways, all these moving parts add complexity to taxable investing. But an investment strategy, designed and executed with forethought and care, will minimize the adverse impact, and maximize the upside with high probability of success.

Taxable investors and their advisors have tools at their disposal, some of them low cost and quite straightforward, to increase net-of-tax-and-fee returns. Understanding how to create better odds of success, where to look for higher magnitude, how to measure risk symmetries and how to retain a higher proportion of profits creates additional benefit. That understanding also will encourage advisors and their taxable clients to ignore vast areas of the investment ecosystem. Most hedge funds, most credit-driven funds, most real estate funds, and most actively managed equity funds are structurally unattractive for taxable investors, even if they make sense for tax-exempt ones. A reduced universe of investment options makes investing easier for us by tightening our focus exclusively onto those opportunities that have the best odds of adding value net of taxes and fees.

KEY CHAPTER TAKEAWAYS

- Taxable investors should evaluate the symmetry of risk, magnitude of profit, probability of winning, and profit retention rates from their unique perspective.
- Given all their differences, managing taxable and tax-exempt portfolios using the same investment theories, the same analysis, the same structures, the same metrics of performance, is not acceptable. We taxable investors need to think and act differently than tax-exempt investors, and our advisors should too.
- The character of profit determines the rate at which it is taxed and when it is taxed. It's important to understand the differences.
- For taxable investors, the more successful an investment becomes, the more expensive it is to sell and the harder it is to replace. Over time, each buy and sell decision becomes more and more important.
- Costs also affect taxable profits. Many investment funds are structurally more attractive to tax-exempt investors than to taxable ones. Avoid them and focus on a smaller and more sensible set of options.

CHAPTER TWO

Diversify at the Right Time and in the Right Way

M ost people think of "diversification" as a financial investment strategy – what percent of stocks, bonds, hedge
funds, private equity, venture capital, and real assets should com-
prise an investment portfolio? But before any of us has the opportunity to think about this aspect of diversification, first we have to
accumulate wealth. That almost always requires long-term, concentrated investments of effort and capital. This chapter explains
how and when to turn concentrated wealth accumulation into
cash for potential reinvestment into that diversified portfolio of
financial assets.

Most talented, ambitious people start their professional lives
with minimal assets, often some debt, minimal earnings, and lots
of earning potential. You can think of that earning potential as a
large but intangible asset. Over time that intangible asset changes
form. Earning potential converts into actual earnings that can be

used to eliminate debts and pay living costs. Whatever earnings are left over convert into savings – a tangible asset.

In addition to receiving salaries, some people are compensated with concentrated ownership in one company through stock, restricted stock, and stock options. Equity in this form can offer great benefits for entrepreneurs, leaders, and managers in growing companies, but it isn't very liquid, and its value will follow the company's fortunes. In other words, it's risky.

In professions like dentistry, teaching, and many others, where reasonably predictable careers provide reasonably predictable cash flow but little opportunity to "equitize" professional skill, saving cash earnings is the only way to build financial assets and to diversify personal balance sheets. The earlier the saving process begins, the longer the savings can compound and the larger they can grow. Professional athletes, actors, authors, and others whose earnings are lumpy should save particularly heavily during high earning periods because their future earning potential is unpredictable.

Regardless of career path, at early career stages, savings should be earmarked largely for growth in a diversified portfolio of equities. A significant chunk of that savings can and should benefit from being locked into tax-advantaged retirement plans. In a traditional retirement plan, earnings are contributed pretax. Within the plan assets grow tax-free, sometimes for many decades. Only when assets are withdrawn will earned income tax be payable. In "Roth" plans, taxes are paid currently on contributed earnings, but within the plan assets grown tax-free and there is no tax due upon withdrawal.[1] Investing in Roth plans is particularly advantageous when your current tax rate is low and when you expect to have higher earnings in later years that put you in higher tax brackets. Roth plan assets are not only protected from higher future tax brackets, they are also protected from future legisled tax hikes.

As an incentive to save more, many corporations will match their employees' contributions to retirement plans up to a specific

---

[1] Early withdrawals from retirement plans, currently legislated as before age 59 ½, may trigger both standard taxes and penalties. Plus, the withdrawn assets lose the potential to continue growing without tax. So savers should consider assets contributed to retirement plans as inaccessible even if they are invested in liquid securities like stocks, bonds, mutual funds, and ETFs.

level. If your firm offers this benefit, your decision to save more actually earns you extra compensation. It's as close to free money as most of us ever get and it will compound tax-free for decades. Take full advantage of that benefit if it's available.

Higher earners may need to put some of their savings in taxable accounts because there are caps on how much they can contribute each year to retirement plans. In this way, they not only diversify their assets, they diversify tax rates on the profits generated by those assets. We will delve more deeply into both points later.

As successful careers develop, the shift from intangible assets to tangible assets accelerates. For those who mostly earn income, or receive dividends from concentrated stock positions, regular addition to savings enables you not only to grow financial assets, it causes you to invest those assets in all kinds of market conditions. Sometimes markets are strong and getting stronger. Sometimes they are about to crack into a bear market. Sometimes you invest near the bottom of the market cycle. Since it is very difficult to optimally time when to add money to financial markets, regular contributions over years and decades lower the risk and add "time diversification."

Time diversification is good for another reason. You gain experience managing financial assets, first with small amounts of money and then larger ones. You learn to work with, and to assess, financial advisors. You gain experience evaluating your own attitudes towards risk through market ups and downs. Do you see market downturns as opportunity to buy good assets at lower prices or do they cause you to lose confidence in your financial strategy and in the people you work with to execute it?

When you own a concentrated position in a business there are several ways to diversify. You can use excess cash flow to diversify and grow within your business – geographically, by customer type, by product; through organic growth or by acquisition. Alternatively, you can distribute excess cash flow in the form of regular dividends or periodic refinancing proceeds to diversify outside the business, including into financial assets. Lastly, you can diversify by selling all or a portion of the business, paying capital gains taxes and reinvesting the net proceeds.

Deciding when and how to sell your concentrated position can be a major strategic and emotional decision, not just straightforwardly financial. Selling enables you to diversify your assets and build a nest egg independent of the business's success, but it's not a costless or riskless decision. This form of diversification comes with big tax payments. In the special case where you sell a big chunk of a business, you could lose control of a cherished enterprise and need to replace income streams that you had enjoyed.

One of the most important things my senior colleagues and I do is to help our clients think strategically across the business, financial, and cultural dimensions of their situation when making big decisions like this. We help them to prepare for sale, to identify presale estate and charitable planning opportunities, and to design a process to maximize value. Careful economic analysis of the timing, benefits, and risks of each pathway (concentration versus diversification), as well as thoughtful discussion of the impact on a family's culture, should not to be taken lightly. There are also questions of how to replace the economic engine and the cash flow that it generates, especially after the government has extracted a big tax bite out of the sale proceeds.

In other words, think twice before selling your business interests. A few years ago, I gave a lecture at Harvard Business School (HBS) reunions. Within a minute of explaining why thinking twice before selling was a good idea, I could feel the cell phone in my pocket vibrate. The text message said, "Please, can we talk today." After my lecture, we spoke for thirty minutes. It turns out the person who reached out had received what felt like a generous unsolicited offer to buy his business, and he had signed the letter of intent to sell without thinking through the implications. Listening to me, he realized this was a big mistake.

There are certainly business and personal considerations associated with the decision to sell. But it is also important to think deeply about tax and estate planning opportunities and risks. Considering sale to an unaffiliated strategic or financial buyer when financial markets are ebullient, the business is performing well, and valuations are high, can be advantageous. In contrast, if you want to transfer assets from one generation in your family to the next, it's generally to your advantage to do so when valuations are near cyclical lows. It is also wise to utilize estate planning techniques when your equity is illiquid, and the business has not been optimized for maximum sale value. And there are tax consequences, especially with outright sale, not the least of which is, do you close the sale in late December or early in January the following year? If you decide to sell, are you prepared to reinvest the sale proceeds? Do you reinvest them all at once or over time? How will you replace the income you generated from your concentrated equity position after you've paid all those taxes? If you're a founder or inheritor of a family business, what will be the emotional and cultural impact on you and the family of selling the business? These are critical questions this HBS entrepreneur hadn't asked until he was deep into the sales process.

During the sale of a family business there are especially large planning implications. Selling a business outright may be exactly the right thing to do, but be prepared for the consequences across business, financial, and cultural dimensions. Some entrepreneurs and business owners feel a vacuum in their purpose and family culture after the business is sold. The fiscal responsibility imposed from the illiquidity of owning and operating a business can evaporate upon sale. Finally, many sellers of businesses have neither the experience, nor the infrastructure, nor the technical skills, nor the passion or inclination to manage a substantial bolus of cash. Liquidity events reduce risk in some ways, but they increase it in others.

Upon learning that someone is selling their business, it's natural and courteous to offer one's congratulations. But be prepared for an unexpected reply from self-aware sellers. "Why are you congratulating me? Yesterday I knew what business I was in. Today, I am in the investment business and I know nothing about it."

In my experience, the challenge goes deeper. The instincts one develops to succeed in business are often contrary to the intuition one builds to succeed as an investor. Most successful business operators allocate capital to their winners, they aren't contrarians, and they are highly sensitized to momentum. They focus on what has worked and do more of it. They cut their losses quickly. Revenue growth, operating margins, return on invested capital, and cash flow are key metrics of success. Whether their company stock is public – with minute-to-minute pricing – or private, they know instinctively that long-term business performance can be disconnected from the stock price for extended periods.

Translating that mindset to investing is challenging. Business operators are inclined to get investment timing wrong because they are more sensitized to momentum than to value or growth at a reasonable price. Many find that being a contrarian is constitutionally challenging. They view turbulent financial markets as a reason to disengage rather than an environment to seek opportunity. In addition, like most of the rest of us, they have selective memories and prefer to focus on their winners, not their losers. It's certainly the winners that get talked about, but without measuring aggregate results it's easy to be left with the impression that investing is easier and more successful than it really is. Time and again I observe highly disciplined businesspeople fall into the trap of not sufficiently measuring the aggregate results of their financial investments. It's as if they don't want to know.

A subset of business sellers will pursue new businesses or other opportunities for focused investments that can be replacement engines for growth. Those new business pursuits do have significant failure risk, no matter how skilled the entrepreneur. So, for these "serial entrepreneurs," I advise allocating a portion of the sale proceeds, ideally enough for a secure retirement, to diversified financial assets, managed according to the tenets in this book's first seven chapters. One business success does not guarantee the second one.

The first step on the road to success as a taxable investor is to build a wealth creation engine, almost invariably through concentrated efforts of time and capital. This chapter discussed key factors in diversifying some of the fruits of that effort into financial assets. For most people, accumulating financial assets is all about consistent saving and investing over many decades. It's about discipline and persistence. For a few, there is one highly impactful liquidity event, or at most a few events. In the latter case, making a timely transition, efficiently and effectively, is no small feat. There are many business, financial, and cultural factors to consider along the way – including investment, tax, and estate planning – to set yourself up to be a successful taxable investor in financial assets. Before we really dig into managing financial assets, we have one additional crucial topic to discuss that relates to everyone who has or will enjoy financial success. That topic is managing deferred tax liabilities.

KEY CHAPTER TAKEAWAYS

- A successful career converts the intangible asset of future promise into the tangible assets of income and, sometimes, business ownership.
- Regardless of career path, saving money early and consistently, and investing it in a disciplined, diversified manner is the most predictable method of building to a secure retirement.
- Business owners have a few ways to diversify: 1) they can do so within their business; 2) they can reinvest excess cash flow, including dividends or refinancing proceeds outside their business into diversifying assets, including financial assets; or 3) they can diversify by selling all or a portion of the business, paying capital gains taxes and reinvesting the net proceeds.
- Think twice before selling your business. Before deciding, carefully consider not only your current circumstances but also what will likely happen in the months and years after selling – across business, financial, and cultural dimensions.

---◆---

CHAPTER THREE

Generate Value from That Magical Liability: Deferred Tax

Most of us start our careers with no equity ownership, no profits, and no deferred taxes. As we build savings, we have the opportunity to invest. Successful investments, whether in a diversified portfolio or in a concentrated position, will experience a widening gap between their cost and their market values. A component of that gap is deferred tax that will have to be paid to the government upon sale of the asset. Deferred tax liabilities may feel amorphous, but they are really good, maybe even a touch magical.

To quote from my first book, *Wealth*:

> *It's like getting no-interest loans from the government! It also has some other attractive features. First, at no point does the government have the authority to say, "We are calling your loan." You have the right to let the free "loan" continue unpaid for as*

17

long as you want, so long as you don't sell the underlying asset.
Second, in most cases, the size of the loan varies proportionately
with the success of the investment. The bigger the gain, the bigger
the loan.

It's easiest to understand the power of deferred tax through
the example of a single equity position in a successful business. So
long as you hold that equity position, it doesn't generate realized
capital gains and taxes are deferred year after year. The longer you
hold it, the more you defer the tax liability associated with selling.
If the company is growing in value, the associated deferred tax
liability grows with it.

As that successful business matures, it creates opportunities to
generate cash through bonus payments, dividends, and recapital-
izations. These may be taxable events, but they create the opportunity to diversify into financial assets. The same concept of building
deferred tax liabilities applies to long-term holdings in a stock
portfolio.

Deferred taxes can grow to have a big impact on your personal finances and the strategies and tactics for managing them.
To keep track, you should reflect them as a liability on your personal balance sheet. To understand why, look at Figure 3.1. Someone with business assets valued at $10 million and a cost of $2
million, index funds worth $6 million and a cost of $1.8 million, a tax-deferred retirement plan of $2 million, and a Roth
IRA of $1 million might think of herself as having a net worth of
$19 million. But that is an incomplete calculation. In the example
shown in the figure, although assets are worth $19 million, the
owner's equity is $15.13 million. The difference, originating from
highly appreciated assets and taxes payable on future distributions
on the tax-deferred retirement plan, is deferred tax liability.[1]

In this example, when the business and the index fund pay
dividends on the $16 million in assets, the entire dividend pay-
ment goes to the owner, including the dividends on the $3.05
million of deferred tax liability (which is unpaid and therefore

[1]A deferred tax liability for you is a deferred tax asset for the federal government,
and maybe your state and local governments.

F I G U R E   3.1   PERSONAL BALANCE SHEET FOR A TAXABLE INVESTOR.

Assets		Liabilities and Owners Equity	
Equity Index Fund(s)	$ 6,000,000	Index Fund Deferred Tax	$ 1,050,000
Business ownership	$10,000,000	Business Deferred Tax	$ 2,000,000
Tax-Deferred Retirement Plan	$ 2,000,000	Retirement Plan Deferred Tax	$ 840,000
Roth IRA	$ 1,000,000	Roth IRA Deferred Tax	$ 0
		Total Deferred Tax	**$ 3,890,000**
		Owner's Equity	**$ 15,110,000**
Total Assets	**$ 19,000,000**	**Owner's Equity & Liabilities**	**$ 19,000,000**

still invested).[2] Likewise, the gross assets in both retirement plans compound while they remain inside but distributions from the tax-deferred retirement plan are taxed as income. Distributions from the Roth IRA are not taxed so there is no deferred tax liability. All the owner's gross assets compound as if there is no deferred tax liability, and the owner gets most of the benefit. If the assets decline in value, so does the deferred tax liability; the government shares the risk (except in the Roth IRA).

There is great benefit in deferring taxes, but the taxes will come due each time you decide to sell an appreciated asset or take a withdrawal from your tax-deferred savings account. You will only be able to reinvest or spend the net proceeds, the amount remaining after paying taxes on your realized gains. The more successful you are at deferring taxes (and therefore, the bigger the deferred liability you create), the harder it will be to replace those assets and the returns they generate after you've sold.

[2] I assume a 25% federal plus state capital gains tax rate on business and mutual fund gains and a 42% federal plus state income tax rate on future distributions from the tax-deferred retirement plan. Zero tax is payable on distributions from the Roth IRA.

In Figure 3.1, let's look at the business ownership in greater detail. The stock representing that ownership has a cost basis of $2 million, a value of $10 million, and a 2% dividend. You have to decide whether to hold your stock, which you expect to generate a total return (dividends plus growth of principal) of 7% over the ensuing decade, or to sell it and reinvest the proceeds in a different company with a 9% expected total return and the same 2% dividend yield. What should you do? If you hold, your $10 million asset will grow and pay a proportionately growing dividend each year. If you sell, the $8 million of profit is taxed at 25%, leaving you with after-tax proceeds of $2 million cost plus $6 million ($8 million profit minus tax of 25% times $8 million) in after-tax profit, for a total of $8 million net. You then invest the $8 million in the second company. Since both investments generate a 2% dividend, in dollar terms the first investment, if held, pays a $200,000 dividend day one: the second pays only $160,000. There is a difference of $40,000, or 25%. Even if the new investment generates a 9% annualized return, thus matching the market value of the first stock at end of the decade, the dividends distributed over that decade from the new, better-performing stock fall 27% short of the dividends paid from the old, theoretically unsold, $10 million asset. On the other hand, depending on which path you went down 10 years before, you prospectively own a stock with a cost basis of $2 million, or one with a cost basis of $8 million and a proportionately lower deferred tax liability. (See Figure 3.2 for a graphic representation.)

Of course, those future returns will not pan out precisely as projected. Nevertheless, it's instructive to illustrate the tradeoffs of trying to decide whether to sell one appreciated security to buy another, or to sell a business and invest the after-tax proceeds in financial assets. It also illustrates why it might make sense for one investor to sell a stock to buy a different one while another investor, with the same knowledge about the tradeoffs, decides not to sell, simply because of the difference in their tax positions. You can do a comparable analysis when considering the sale of a mutual fund, an ETF, or any other type of financial asset.

It's important to think about the consequences of selling in the face of rising asset values, but what if asset prices fall? Capital

F I G U R E   **3.2**   **T O S E L L O R T O H O L D ?**

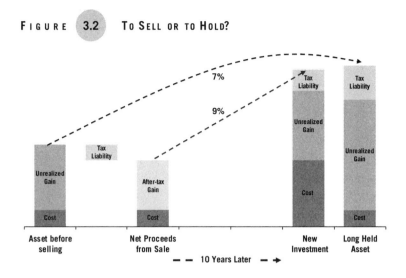

gains taxes are payable on realized profits, not on assets. Why does this matter? When the values of appreciated securities fall, the government suffers a disproportionate percentage of the decline. In this example, if your $10 stock falls 50% in value, the deferred tax liability drops 63% while your owner's net worth drops 47%. (If the cost basis were zero instead of $2, the declines would be proportional.) On the other hand, if you sold, and the newly purchased $8 stock fell by half, you would have an unrealized loss of $4. You could sell the stock and realize the loss to shield other realized gains if you have them, but what if you don't? You cannot "claw back" the taxes you paid on the sale of your stock unless the gain and the loss are realized in the same calendar year. You would have to "carry forward" the loss until you realized new gains. Meanwhile inflation and the time-value of money eat into the value of the unused loss carryforward.

Whenever you consider selling larger positions in low basis stock, do this analysis. Even though it is an exercise in precision over accuracy, it is still instructive. Look at the numbers and ask yourself, is it worth selling? How confident am I that a new investment will perform that much better? If I need the dividends to finance lifestyle, how will I replace them with after-tax dollars, both immediately post-sale and years into the future? Is there a life event or estate planning opportunity that should cause me to delay a decision to get a stepped-up basis? If the reinvested proceeds decline in value, can I use the losses to offset other taxable gains? When you evaluate replacement value proactively, this discipline naturally raises the bar to selling and incentivizes you to think and act with a long-term focus, whether or not, after careful analysis, you decide to sell.

Doing the analysis will give you pause – healthy pause – and in some cases will lead you to conclude not to sell. In my family, I don't think this analysis was ever seriously done before the decision to sell Carnation to Nestlé was made. If the powers-that-be had done so, maybe we would not have sold and Carnation would still be an independent, thriving business.

Sometimes selling and paying the tax is exactly the right thing to do. Don't fall into the trap of thinking you shouldn't ever sell simply because an investment has been successful and has created a large deferred tax liability. With an eye to the long term, keeping tabs on the fundamentals of any business or financial investment is essential.

In contrast to those of us who pay taxes, tax-exempt investors don't have the same incentives or constraints to be long-term builders of businesses and investors in equities. Particularly as transaction costs have collapsed in the last two decades, it costs them virtually nothing to be traders. They don't have a government partner with aligned incentives. They can trade with impunity if it improves measured returns and increases year-end bonuses. The effects are obvious when looking at daily turnover volumes in the major stock exchanges. In private equity and real estate funds the effects are more subtle but also material.

ALTERNATIVES TO SELLING

Some built-in rigidity works well for long-term taxable investors, but we also need a balance. Fortunately, we have a tool at our disposal to balance the incentives imbedded in deferred taxes with the ability to defer or defray some costs of selling: a line of credit. It can be prudent to incorporate modest, intermittent leverage in your diversified investment portfolios. Drawing on a line of credit in this way enables you to make investments without having to realize gains from the sale of appreciated assets, especially ones you consider undervalued. Access to credit when most investors are fearful is particularly useful. When markets recover you can look for options to pay down the debt, pay taxes when reinvestment opportunities are less compelling, and "reload" for the next great opportunities, whenever they arise.

Prudence and restraint are key here. If you aggressively draw on your credit line relative to your collateral, a market dip may cause you to face a margin call at the worst possible time. Not only could you find that you must liquidate assets (that have declined in value) to meet the margin call, but the very process of liquidation could trigger tax payments, adding insult to injury. Paradoxically, the more successful your tax deferral program, the greater these tax payments could be.

In the same vein of thinking, I recommend against drawing on a credit line to meet spending requirements. Drawing on the line to support spending would reduce available margin, diminish your flexibility, and make your portfolio more susceptible to irrecoverable shocks. Instead, to finance spending above and beyond dividends, sell assets and pay any associated taxes. Don't borrow for this purpose.

For those who own large concentrated positions in one or more public equities, other techniques to diversify exist. These include using the derivative securities strategies built around options and "collars" (including "Prepaid Variable Forwards") that can be designed to hedge some of the downside risk of your position, but they may also limit upside.[3] It may also be possible to

---

[3] For more information here are two references to articles about various approaches to managing concentrated stock positions and their associated risks. They were both published some years ago, but they provide useful overviews. There have been some changes since these articles were published, including shortening the period of illiquidity of Exchange Funds, so if you wish to pursue any of these strategies in greater detail please consult your tax and financial advisors to get the most up to date information and to help evaluate if any of these options are right for you. http://www .twenty-first.com/pdf/boczar_imca.pdf and http://www.alliancebernstein.com/Research-Publications/CMA-created-content/PrivateClient/PDFs/2389_TheEnviable Dilemma_BB.pdf.

participate in an Exchange Fund where you and others contribute your concentrated positions to a new investment vehicle, sharing the risk and the upside of all contributed securities combined. Charitable Remainder Trusts can also be established to offload some of the risk, essentially converting the asset into a stream of current income while contributing residual assets to a designated charitable organization. Each of these techniques involves incremental costs, subtle but substantial risks, potential for illiquidity, and complex tax rules that must be stringently adhered to. These important details are beyond the scope of this book but should be familiar to financial advisors. If you make the right assessments and follow the rules, the results can be gratifying.

KEY CHAPTER TAKEAWAYS

- Deferred taxes offer a great opportunity. You earn profits from them and they help to defray risk. You don't pay interest on them and they aren't callable. The government is a uniquely constructive investment partner in this way.
- When considering whether to sell a highly appreciated asset, estimate the tax impact and the return required from the replacement investment in order to break even. This exercise highlights the economic incentive for taxable investors to think and act long term and to ride out the interim volatility that is inherent in investing.
- Consider a credit line as a tool for disciplined management of deferred taxes.

Chapter Four

If You Want Wealth to Grow, Own Stocks

The power of compounding may feel as amorphous as deferring tax, but it is even more powerful. The two concepts are also inextricably linked for taxable investors. Growing $1,000 at a 4% rate from age 20 to age 70 years generates $7,107. If the growth rate is 8%, one ends up with $46,902. 8% instead of 4% doesn't double one's assets over 50 years, it multiplies them by 6.6 times. Long-term after-tax rates of return matter, enormously. That is why this chapter is so important.

Once you've started building a base of diversified financial assets, the easiest and highest-probability way to generate a solid after-tax growth rate is to buy and hold a basket of stocks for decades. The easiest and highest probability way to build a top-performing equity portfolio is for that basket to track a broad market index. Indexing is neither a new nor a controversial concept. Many of the most experienced investors, from Warren Buffett to David Swensen to the late Jack Bogle, advise all but the most sophisticated investors to index their publicly traded equities. I agree, and the evidence broadly supports the advice.[1] It is very difficult, even for trained professionals, to determine in advance which of the thousands of stocks to choose among will grow faster than average and which will fall short. Plus, in the quest for better returns, every time you sell a stock to buy another one, you generate tax impact. Buying a broad market index obviates the need to make those inherently risky selections, the portfolio suffers minimal taxable turnover, and the fees associated with owning the index are very low.

This simple approach is even more compelling for taxable investors than for tax-exempt institutions. What is so powerful about owning a broad-based index like the S&P 500, a developed markets equity index, or even an all-country world index that includes emerging markets equities, is *the structural opportunity to compound profits and defer taxes for a long time.* Let's explore why this approach is compelling.

OVER TIME, STOCKS OUTPERFORM BONDS

It is common knowledge that over the long run, broad-based equity indexes have outperformed bonds, cash, and gold on a

---

[1] Here is just a small sampling of data and experts evaluating the success of active management:

Charles D. Ellis, *Winning the Loser's Game: Timeless Strategies for Successful Investing,* 7th ed. (McGraw Hill, 2017), Chapter 1.

"Evaluation of Active Managers' Performance Through a Risk Lens," Risk Adjusted SPIVA Scorecard, December 13, 2018, https://www.institutionalinvestor.com/article/b1bf6tj1ftk0sp/evaluation-of-active-managers-performance-through-a-risk-lens.

Not only do active managers have a hard time beating their benchmarks, but the ones who do outperform over a period of time have a really hard time maintaining that excess performance. Manager performance has strong "mean reverting" characteristics, meaning that those that have performed well tend to struggle in the future. S&P Dow Jones research documents this tendency in "Does Past Performance Matter: The Persistence Scorecard," contributed to by Berlinda Liu, CFA, and Aye M. Soe, CFA, December 2018. Unfortunately, since many people chase past performance, they tend to buy high and sell low. This is not a good way to make money.

pretax basis. After tax and after inflation, the difference is nothing short of dramatic.

The profits on stocks, whether individual or as part of an indexed portfolio, are usually taxed at a lower rate than on taxable bonds (tax-exempt bonds have lower coupons than their taxable equivalents, essentially pricing in the tax rate impact). Stock dividends are taxed at a lower rate than bond coupons, and they generally represent a lower percentage of total return. Consequently, most of the tax on bonds is due every year, whereas for stocks the majority can be deferred until the stock is sold at a profit. If you hold stocks for the long term, capital gains tax can be deferred for years or decades, allowing your returns to compound and creating a deferred tax liability. If you never sell, tax may never be paid on capital gains. Simply put, equities owned for the long run benefit enormously from the power of compounding in taxable portfolios. Bonds don't. Cash doesn't.

Jeremy Siegel, the Russell E. Palmer Professor of Finance at Wharton School of the University of Pennsylvania and author of the influential book *Stocks for the Long Run,* calculated the long-term, inflation-adjusted, after-tax returns of stocks, bonds, and cash.[2] The chosen start date for this data series was 1913 because it is the year the US federal income tax was first instituted. For investors in the top marginal tax bracket and realizing capital gains every year, stocks generated a 2.7% annualized real (adjusted for inflation) after-tax return. Bonds lost 0.3% per year; cash lost 2.3% per year. If investors deferred their capital gains or were in lower tax brackets, the relative advantage of stocks increased.

On the surface it doesn't sound like much difference. Nevertheless, Siegel's work piqued my interest in this relative advantage. Top marginal rates on interest income have generally trended down from high levels during World War II. Top rates for long-term capital gains have ranged in a narrow band mostly between 20 and 30%.[3] Historic tax trends would advantage

[2] Jeremy J. Siegel, *Stocks for the Long Run: The Definitive Guide to Financial Market Returns and Long-Term Investment Strategies* (McGraw Hill Education, 2014), pp. 135–136.
[3] Ibid, p. 134.

bonds more today relative to history because of the narrowing differentials between taxes on income and capital gains. But, two other factors favor stocks. The first is that since 2003 dividends have been taxed at long-term capital gains rates, not income rates. Second, investors don't need to sell their equities every year, enabling the stocks to compound tax-deferred so long as they are not sold.

Figure 4.1 analyzes the real (inflation-adjusted) returns of US stocks, global stocks, 10-year US Treasury Bonds, and US Treasury Bills. To these long-term results, I applied a 2% inflation rate (the Fed's current target inflation rate) because taxes are applied to nominal profits, not real profits. I then applied the current federal tax rate to demonstrate how the power of compounding and the ability to design tax deferral into an equity investment program impact the real growth of after-tax profits over 30 years. Using these assumptions, USstocks outperform bonds by more than 200 times, global stocks perform 100 times better and they both beat cash by even more. Those are huge differences. (For the numbers, see Figure 4.1.)

The outperformance of the stock market relative to these other asset classes is remarkably consistent over shorter time frames, too. Figure 4.2 shows the estimated real pretax returns of US stocks and ten-year US Treasury Bonds from 1946 to 2018 over rolling five-year and 20-year periods. Referring to the construct at the beginning of Chapter 1, the success rate has been high. In rolling five-year periods, stocks outperformed bonds 78% of the time before tax. The preferred tax treatment of a well-structured equity portfolio relative to bonds would increase that success rate significantly. In addition, the equity return profiles have been asymmetric and the magnitudes high; stocks mostly outperformed by a lot and underperformed modestly. Over rolling 20-year periods, stocks have outperformed 100% of the time, before factoring in the better tax treatment of stocks. Even looking at one-year periods, stocks outperformed bonds more than two-thirds of the time before considering taxes. In Figure 4.2, observe how much less volatile the 20-year rolling equity returns are than over

FIGURE 4.1   THE POWERFUL IMPACT OF ASSET CLASS SELECTION
ON COMPOUNDING AFTER-TAX RETURNS.[4]

	Annualized Pretax Real Return	Pretax Return Assuming 2% Inflation	Federal 2018 Tax Rate Applied	Real Growth of $100 After 30 Years[5]
US Stocks (1926–2018)	6.8%	8.8%	23.8%	$1,008
Global Stocks (1969–2018)	4.4%	6.4%	23.8%	411
10-Year Treasury Bonds (1942–2018)	1.5%	3.5%	40.8%	4
Treasury Bills (1942–2018)	0.1%	2.1%	40.8%	−37

five years, and how similarly flat they appear relative to bonds. Plus, on a rolling 20-year basis, only stocks always made money on an inflation-adjusted basis.

[4] The US Stocks figures are calculated based on data from S&P500 Value Weighted Return ©2019 Center for Research in Security Prices (CRSP) and for 10-Year Treasury Bonds and Treasury Bills from Treasury Bills, Bonds, Inflation © Center for Research in Security Prices (CRSP), The University of Chicago Booth School of Business. Global Stocks data is from the MSCI World Index sourced through Bloomberg, Inc. The starting year was determined by the available data. The source of tax rates is "2018 Aperio Tax Guide for Investment Decisions," Aperio Group, LLC and Marketwatch.com. Tax rates do not account for withholding taxes on foreign investments or state or local taxes.

[5] I use the following assumptions to calculate the real value of $100 after 30 years invested in each asset class. For equities there is a 2% dividend that is taxed currently with after-tax proceeds reinvested. All capital gains are deferred and not taxed after 30 years. Bonds and bills have their entire nominal return taxed at the stated tax rate each year. This is admittedly a simplified set of assumptions. Tax rates have varied greatly historically, and they will change again. Dividend yields also go up and down, as do the splits between income and capital gains in fixed income. Inflation can also be volatile. The goal is to be directionally reasonable to point out the huge disparity of long-term after-tax performance of these asset classes. Changing the assumptions in all but draconian ways does not change the fundamental conclusion. (Past performance is no guarantee of future returns. The performance of an index is not an exact representation of any particular investment, as you cannot invest directly in an index.)

FIGURE  4.2   LONG-TERM ROLLING REAL RETURNS FOR STOCKS AND
                        BONDS.[6]

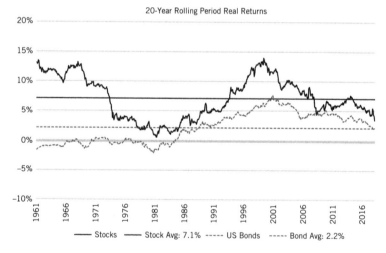

[6]Both 5-year and 20-year charts are derived using data from *S&P500 Value Weighted Return* ©2019 Center for Research in Security Prices (CRSP) and for 10-year Treasuries from *Treasury Bills, Bonds, Inflation* © Center for Research in Security Prices (CRSP), University of Chicago Booth School of Business.

GEOGRAPHIC DIVERSIFICATION

I advise equity investors to invest globally. There are many great companies, many geopolitical crosscurrents, and myriad other factors that create risk and opportunity around the world that global businesses generally manage to good effect, with occasional exceptions. Global investors get more diversification and more opportunity. In the last decade the US stock market (including US-headquartered global businesses) has outperformed the rest of the world, and with good reason. But there are other periods when the reverse has been true and will be again.

The United States has inherent advantages. Geographic benefits include long navigable internal waterways, tremendous and diverse natural resources, eastern and western borders that are protected by thousands of miles of ocean, and relatively non-threatening neighbors to the south and north. It is in a temperate climate. The country has large quantities of fertile soil and fresh water; it is relatively uncrowded and has more favorable demographics than many countries. As the largest and most diverse economy in the world, it is less dependent on foreign markets than most and it controls the world's reserve currency. Our military is strong. The rule of law largely prevails, and government institutions are strong. University and government research resources are deep. Furthermore, the incredibly entrepreneurial cultures of Silicon Valley and other hot spots around the country drive innovation at unprecedented pace. Plus, for many of you, it is your home country.

Although I am a global investor, I strategically overweight the US. There is no exact science for determining the right answer – and of course the answer for you will be heavily determined by the totality of your own particular circumstance. But investing 75% of your equity allocation in a global equity index that is roughly 55% US and 45% other developed countries and emerging markets, and adding to that position another 25% in a broad-based US equity index is not a bad option. It invests approximately two-thirds of your equities in US companies and one-third non-US As you think about the right geographic mix, don't forget to consider what geographic regions of the world your career or business is most dependent on. Think about whether your real estate or private equity investments are predominantly or exclusively US oriented. These factors make international exposure more important for diversification, and in some cases could cause you to tilt your indexed exposure more heavily outside the US For example, the indexed components of most of my clients' assets are indexed globally, without adding a separate US indexed overweight, because the rest of their business and financial assets are already US dominant.

MANAGING SHORT-TERM VOLATILITY

A counterargument to having an equity-oriented portfolio is that stocks are risky, riskier than many other asset classes. Measured over a standard one-year time horizon, that is true. And the tightness one feels in one's gut during a market swoon is tangible. But many investors, maybe even most, have a longer time horizon than one or even five years. In Chapter 5, we will explore what happens to risk when you employ longer-term thinking.

To complement a long-term core equity position, investors should turn to high quality taxable and tax-exempt short-term bonds and cash to meet anticipated planned spending, a potential dip in dividend payments, and unexpected emergencies.[7] They need added certainty for nearer-term requirements or high spending rates. If under age 59½ they will want to own these assets directly, not in a retirement plan, so they can access the funds without penalty. For this portion of their investments, maybe up to 10% of the total depending on need, they should be willing to trade away the positive asymmetry of stocks for the more stable return of fixed income even though high-quality bonds have

---

[7]For example, some tax-exempt investors buy long-term US Treasury Bonds as "disaster insurance." They are willing to accept a lower overall return in exchange for safety. But remember, because they are tax-exempt, they don't pay 40% of bond coupons back to the government. For you, the economics are less favorable. At current interest rates, whatever capital you may invest is likely to decline in real value and there are easily imagined scenarios where both stocks and bonds – even Treasury Bonds – could lose value. So, the insurance is an imperfect hedge to a declining equity market. Only in a deflationary market is the insurance likely to pay off.

negative asymmetry and generate little or no real, after-tax profit. If all goes according to plan, investors receive their coupons and ultimately their principal. Since 1982, declining interest rates have also provided a tailwind for bond performance. But with interest rates as low as they are today, that tailwind is pretty much tapped out and it could become a headwind if a secular rise in rates occurs. In addition, low coupon payments are causing investors to reach for higher yields at the risk of lower credit quality. Now, without an interest rate tail wind and additional credit risk, indexing bonds could leave you exposed. That's one reason why I don't recommend indexing them. Investors who choose to invest in bonds should seek a low-cost credit-conscious manager of investment grade fixed income and cash. Good credit analysis in bond portfolios helps to reduce risk, and that skill can come at a reasonable price, especially when you need it most – at times of economic and market stress.

Some investors and their advisors have become enamored of alternative investments, especially hedge funds, as another way to control risk and generate higher returns. As a rule, hedge funds are terrible vehicles for deferring tax and, as the asset class has grown, most funds have produced disappointing results, even before tax. In short, I advise you, as a taxable investor, to approach hedge funds with skill and skepticism, or not at all. (We will discuss alternative investments in greater detail in Chapter 9.)

ASSET LOCATION: TAXABLE, TAX-DEFERRED, OR TAX-EXEMPT?

When I speak of asset location, I am not speaking of geography in the traditional sense. Taxable investors often structure their financial affairs into various "pots" that each have distinctive characteristics, including the tax rate applied to the investments in that pot. Asset location analysis refers to asking which assets should go into which pots. It is an important component of asset allocation for taxable investors.

Most taxable investors have some financial assets in tax-deferred retirement vehicles such as traditional IRAs, 401(k),

403(b), or Roth versions of the same. You contribute pretax earnings to traditional retirement plans and those dollars compound tax free. However, you pay income tax decades later when you take distributions. In a Roth vehicle you contribute after-tax dollars. Once in the Roth vehicle the assets compound tax free and no tax is due when distributions are made. I own both types of retirement plans.

Most people have periods when they aren't earning much income because of unemployment, going back to school, changing careers, attending to family, or starting a business. If you have an Individual Retirement Account (IRA) or a 401(k)-retirement plan plus some additional savings, take the opportunity of a year with low taxable income to swap your standard IRA or 401(k) into a Roth IRA or 401(k). In effect, you will lock in the low tax rate on the assets you convert and protect them forever against future government tax increases. In addition, the Roth asset will grow tax-free as long as you own it. When you start withdrawing funds from the account, you will pay no tax. With one timely transfer you can save yourself a lot of money and reduce uncertainty around future tax rates.

Since stocks, and especially index funds, are much more tax-efficient than bonds, consider overweighting bonds in your regular retirement vehicles and tax-inefficient but high compounding assets in your Roth. They will compound up to twice as fast inside such vehicles. If you're younger than 59 1/2 you won't be able to withdraw the income or principal without penalty, but at least your coupon income won't be taxed inside the vehicle.[8] Furthermore, when you have assets in taxable, tax-deferred, and

---

[8] For additional information, refer to William Reichenstein, PhD, CFA, and William Meyer, "The Asset Location Decision Revisited," *Journal of Financial Planning* 26 (11), pp. 48–55, and Stephen M. Horan, PhD, CFA, "Applying After-Tax Asset Allocation," *Journal of Wealth Management* (10) 2, pp. 84–93. See also Robert M. Dammon, Chester S. Spatt, and Harold H. Zhang, "Optimal Asset Location and Allocation with Taxable and Tax-Deferred Investing," *Journal of Finance* 59 (2004), pp. 999–1037. There are numerous other studies that show the benefits of putting highly taxed assets into retirement plans and lightly taxed assets in taxable accounts. From other studies of the subject by Gene Amromin and others, it does not appear that most people (or their advisors) heed this advice.

tax-exempt buckets, you are diversifying your exposure to higher tax rates and giving yourself more tools to manage through an uncertain future. Let me give you several examples of what I mean about the benefits of diversifying your tax rates. If you're in a high tax bracket today, realizing capital gains in a traditional retirement plan to make an expenditure triggers a much higher tax rate – because the whole distribution is treated as income – than if you were to sell appreciated stock that you own directly and paying capital gains tax just on your profit. On the other hand, if you are considering such a decision but are in a low tax bracket and over age 59 ½, it may make more sense to take the money from your retirement plan and let your taxable equities continue to compound. Having different "buckets" with different tax rates gives you more tools to manage optimally, both at the times you add to each bucket and at times of withdrawal.

I haven't talked much yet about estate planning but it's possible to create a "grantor trust" for the benefit of someone else; most such trusts are created for children of the grantor but that doesn't have to be the case. These trusts are subject to income and capital gains tax. However, the grantor can choose to pay the tax personally or have the trust pay its own tax. Doing the former helps the grantor to reduce the value of his or her own estate that may otherwise be subject to estate tax and, in so doing, help the grantor trust grow faster in value. This is an option for the grantor, not a requirement, and the decision can be made at the time the tax is due. This choice creates tax optionality and is perfectly legal if proper procedures are followed and documented.

In addition to retirement plans and grantor trusts, there are other common vehicles for diversifying tax rates. 529 education plans allow you to save for education expenses tax efficiently. I particularly like the flexibility of a Donor Advised Fund for philanthropic purposes. You can contribute highly appreciated securities to your DAF in one year, taking a substantial tax deduction, never paying tax on the capital gains, and eliminating the risk that the investment's fortunes reverse. Then, in future years you can make charitable gifts with the proceeds. It's a great planning tool, unlimited in size.

One other asset location decision to consider is the optimal use of the mortgage interest deduction. Most American homeowners take out a mortgage at some point. On new mortgages on primary and/or secondary residences, up to a combined total of $750,000, the interest is tax deductible, with some exceptions. This makes mortgage debt very inexpensive, especially at today's low interest rates. By aspiration and by structure, we are encouraged to pay down our mortgages. However, in the current environment it may be more economic to choose an interest-only mortgage and to add the payment savings to your tax-deferred retirement savings plan.[9]

Later chapters explore additional opportunities to get more creative with financial assets to improve returns and the odds of achieving them. But you don't have to go there right away. Starting simply gives more time to build skills, infrastructure, networks, and other resources to effectively manage your investment portfolio. With additional understanding and confidence, you can then layer on complexity and opportunity with improved chances for success.

KEY CHAPTER TAKEAWAYS

- The government offers taxable investors powerful incentives to be long-term investors in equities. Plus, on a pretax basis stocks have substantially outperformed bonds and cash over time. Adding these two together makes a strong case for being a long-term equity investor, unless you have near-term needs or a high spending rate.
- Invest globally, despite recent US market success. But there are good reasons to do so with a US bias.
- Set aside enough cash for short-term needs. Make sure you can access it without penalty.
- Start simple, with a low-cost, low-turnover, indexed equity portfolio. You can always add complexity in the fullness of time and with insights borne of experience.

[9]Gene Amromin, Jennifer Huang, and Clemens Sialm, "The Tradeoff Between Mortgage Prepayments and Tax-Deferred Retirement Savings," *Journal of Public Economics* 91 (no. 10, 2007), pp. 2014–2040.

- Diversify tax rates and improve net returns through thoughtful asset location: put bonds and other tax-inefficient assets in your regular and Roth IRA, 401(k), or 403(b) and own equities directly. In the current low-interest-rate environment, add to your retirement plan rather than reducing your mortgage.
- In a year when you have low taxable earnings, switch some or all of your traditional IRA or 401(k) into a Roth IRA or Roth 401(k), locking in a low tax rate on the transfer and never paying tax again on those assets.

CHAPTER FIVE

Lengthen Time Horizon to Lower Risk and Enhance Returns

S tocks are less risky than you think. In Chapter 4, we explored the wealth creation potential of a taxable equity portfolio relative to bonds and cash. To me, that alone is a compelling reason to be an equity-oriented investor, even though it's widely viewed that stocks are much riskier than bonds or cash. This perception is based on an investment industry standard measure of risk called the "annual standard deviation of return"; by that standard measure the perception is true – stocks appear much riskier.[1] Measured by annual standard deviation of real return you can see in the left-hand column grouping of Figure 5.1 that stocks have been more than twice as risky as bonds and three

---

[1] Standard deviations are calibrated in percentages and they express the variability of annual returns relative to their average return.

times as risky as T-bills.[2] As you watch the value of your stock portfolio rise and fall day to day, or in any given month or year, your intuition or gut confirms the precise math.

But here is the important kicker: Math is always precise, but the logic behind it isn't always right. Although convenient and widely touted, the one-year time horizon used to measure statistical risk is probably not the right measure for investors who invest for 10, 20, 30 years, or more. The best measure of investment risk is one that approximates *your* investment time horizon. Look at the last two columns of Figure 5.1 to see what happened to the relative risk of owning stocks, bonds, and cash when longer time horizons are applied to the measure of standard deviation. Measured over longer periods, the riskiness of stocks dropped dramatically, to the point that they have been no riskier than bonds or cash and they have consistently generated a lot more profit. If pictures speak more loudly to you than numbers, refer back to Figure 4.2 and notice how much more consistent the returns to stocks have been when measured over five or 20 years on both an absolute basis and relative to bonds. Some investment professionals argue against comparing annualized returns and standard deviations measured over longer periods because small differences

---

[2]Risk here is measured before taking taxes into account. I have not found independent research that explores how to measure standard deviation of return after tax. Thinking about the problem has not brought clarity to the subject. It's clear that the taxation of dividends and interest lowers the upside of those components of return. I think isolating this component of taxation would lower the riskiness of taxable bonds more than stocks because, at least today, interest is taxed at higher rates than dividends. The impact of capital gains tax on risk is another matter. As taxable investors, the government is a partner in our capital gains and our capital losses. The extent to which we realize gains and losses, and can net one against the other, has a big impact on after-tax standard deviation of return. So do the relative tax rates of stocks and bonds and the proportion of their returns that are taxed at each rate. Through the actions that we take as individual investors, there are scenarios where we can significantly decrease downside risk without increasing upside risk of capital gains and losses. All this complexity leads me to the conclusion that trying to calculate a comprehensive picture of after-tax standard deviation of return would create more confusion than enlightenment. Suffice it to say that since the government allows us to offset losses and gains against one another when calculating taxes, it eases some of the pain of loss.

in these figures can translate to big dollar differences over 20 or 30 years. You saw in Figure 4.1 that single-digit differences in annualized pretax returns of stocks and bonds masked the 100+ times difference in dollar values 30 years later. Thus, it's true that if the annualized after-tax returns of stocks over a 20- or 30-year period were even slightly below that of bonds, the adverse dollar impact of investing largely in stocks could be huge. However, you'll notice in the 20-year chart in Figure 4.2 that stocks never underperformed bonds, even before tax. And in many 20-year periods, the outperformance of stocks measured in dollars was huge. Furthermore, Figure 4.2 doesn't account for the fact that by adding to their savings regularly or intermittently throughout their careers and, in retirement, by having some capacity to adjust spending rates downward in tough times, taxable investors can lower the risk of interim stock market declines.[3]

FIGURE 5.1 THE EFFECT OF TIME HORIZON ON STANDARD DEVIATION OF REAL RETURN.[4]

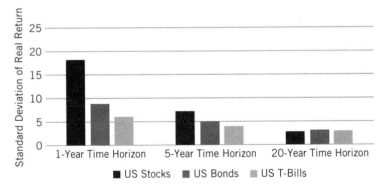

[3]For a contrary perspective, see Lubos Pastor and Robert F. Stambaugh, "Are Stocks Really Less Volatile in the Long Run?" *Journal of Finance*, March 2012. An excerpt from the abstract reads: "we find that stocks are substantially more volatile over long horizons from an investor's perspective."

[4]Measured by standard deviations of average holding-period annual real returns, 1802 to 1996. Source: "Stocks Bonds, the Sharpe Ratio and the Investment Horizon: A comment by Jeremy J. Siegel." *Financial Analysts Journal* 55 (no. 2), p. 2250. Professor Siegel's data in Figure 5.1 covers almost 200 years but it excludes the last

A longer time horizon may be well and good, but in construct-ing asset allocation you should factor in the correlation of asset classes as well as relative risk. If two asset classes are risky and have low correlations to one another, then owning both and being able to rebalance between them is useful. This is a typical argument for owning both stocks and bonds. Unfortunately, in a taxable port-folio, rebalancing – trimming an asset that has done relatively well to buy more of one that has done relatively poorly – often comes at a significant tax cost that negates some or all the rebalancing benefit.

Investors with a longer horizon find that stocks are not only less risky (as shown in the chart), but stocks also become more highly correlated with bonds over longer periods of time, further

22 years. With the able assistance of Robert Seery, a ChicagoBooth MBA student of mine, we derived the chart seen here using data from *S&P500 Value Weighted Return* ©2019 Center for Research in Security Prices (CRSP), and for 10-year Treasuries and US 30-day T-bills from *Treasury Bills, Bonds, Inflation* © Center for Research in Security Prices (CRSP), University of Chicago Booth School of Business. The analysis goes back to January 1, 1926, for stocks and January 1, 1942, for US 30-day US T-bills and US 10-year Treasury Bonds. The analysis and conclusions are similar to Siegel's when analyzing this CRSP database, though T-bills retain the lowest standard deviation throughout. I added a 30-year time horizon to the chart for additional reference, though admittedly it has fewer data points than shorter periods.

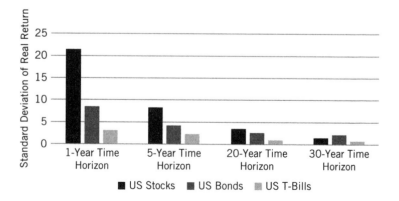

reducing the theoretical benefit of rebalancing.[5] And recall that in Chapter 4 we saw that stocks have consistently performed better than bonds in the long run. In short, if you were able withstand or ignore the short-term swings in equity markets, your persistence has been well rewarded over the long term.[6] I see no fundamental reason for this pattern to change.

It's fair to ask: Do I have a long-term time horizon? Young people saving for retirement and adding regularly to their investment portfolios certainly should. It's why increasingly popular Target Date Funds for folks retiring in 40, 30, 20, even 10 years are mostly invested in equities. Those with volatile or short careers like professional athletes or (most) rock stars need to think and act long-term because their careers are so unpredictable: insufficient savings or excessive spending could result in a hard fall. Even people approaching retirement are likely to be reliant on their savings for decades. Actuarially speaking, there is a one in four chance that at least one member of a couple aged 65 will live to be 94, an additional 29 years.[7]

<hr/>

[5]John Y. Campbell and Luis M. Viceira, "The Term Structure of the Risk-Return Tradeoff." This article explores the relationship of US stock and bond performance at various time horizons. Volatility and correlation are both important factors in determining asset allocation. "Real returns on stocks and fixed-maturity bonds are positively correlated at all horizons but the magnitude of their correlation changes dramatically across investment horizon. At short horizons of a few quarters, correlation is about 20% but it quickly increases to 60% at horizons of about six years and stays above 40% for horizons up to 18 years; at longer horizons, it declines steadily to levels around 15%." In other words, the diversifying benefits of owning stocks and bonds are lower for investors, especially those with time horizons of 6 to 18 years, and over the long run stocks generate much higher returns.

[6]Campbell and Viceira did their analysis based on the total return of stocks with dividends reinvested. So I asked, what happens to these characteristics if dividends are excluded and we only look at the principal return of equities? Again, with the help of Robert Seery, and using data from *S&P500 Value Weighted Return* ©2019 Center for Research in Security Prices (CRSP), University of Chicago Booth School of Business, we assessed performance characteristics of stocks' principal value after removing dividends. Our analysis suggested that stocks behave similarly in the long run, even if dividends were not reinvested.

[7]National Center for Health Statistics, National Vital Statistics System, Mortality, 2015.

Business owners are an interesting case. They almost certainly track daily or weekly sales figures and quarterly or annual retained earnings growth as measures of their business's health, but unless the company is public, they rarely stop to calculate "What is my company worth to a prospective buyer today?" The focus, rightly, is on long-term value creation. When the business is doing well, they are looking for the next opportunity. If it is flagging, they worry. But they rarely contemplate selling the business based on some third-party notion of value, which is largely beyond their control.

In contrast, a portfolio of publicly traded stocks can be priced second-to-second and it's easy to become fixated on those price movements. Certainly, the Wall Street talking heads are. In my experience, business owners (and others) often think stock prices reflect fundamentals. They don't, except in the very long term. The famous professor, author, and investor Benjamin Graham once said, "In the short run, the market is a voting machine but in the long run, it is a weighing machine." We should avoid getting caught up in the voting machine price that happens to be agreed upon by the marginal buyer and the marginal seller at any given moment. Keep your eye on your 10-, 20-, 30-year plan and stay the course.

Very wealthy people or frugal people who expect to share their good fortune with their children and grandchildren, or who have strategic philanthropic intent for their assets, should have an even longer time horizon. Some families with multigenerational wealth talk about having a 100-year view. In these families, the current generation isn't investing for its own well-being; for those with wealth substantially greater than what they will spend in a lifetime, the success or failure of their investment programs won't likely impact their own lifestyles. The impact will be on children or grandchildren (more on that in Chapters 10, 11, and 12).

Of course, some people by circumstance or by disposition do have a shorter-term focus. These investors should manage their portfolios more "conservatively" in the traditional sense. They'll give up a lot of long-term upside, but near-term stability and liquidity are more important to them. And don't forget, the more you spend in excess of your annual earned income, the shorter your time horizon needs to be and the fewer equities you should own.

Many people's time horizons shorten as they enter retirement. This shortening is reflected in how the asset allocation of Target Date Funds become more conservative. Selling stocks to buy more conservative fixed income investments is a straightforward decision inside a deferred tax retirement account because there are no tax implications from selling. However, in taxable portfolios, especially ones with low cost basis, the switching costs are higher. So, in that situation, first, consider rebalancing within your retirement plan. In your taxable accounts, be conscious that you probably have choices about what stocks or mutual fund shares to sell. Investigate the cost and market value of each tax lot. Trading out of ones with smaller embedded gains will lower your tax cost and your reinvestment risk.

When it comes to time horizon, the greatest danger is to think you have a long-time horizon and then through misfortune or, more commonly, in reaction to a deep or extended bear market, you change your mind and shift your asset allocation from stocks to bonds or cash when the market is down; in doing so, you may receive a chunky tax bill, too. One of the benefits of being a taxable investor is that a growing deferred tax liability is a deterrent to this kind of behavior, redoubling your conviction to remain a long-term investor in the face of market volatility. As described in the previous chapter, analyze the impact of selling before you do so. Switching at the wrong time can create an untimely tax bill, lower dividend income, and, worst of all, result in "buying high and selling low," causing you inadvertently to dig yourself into a financial hole from which it is difficult ever to escape.

A second danger to consider is that future tax rate changes are hard to predict but are certainly impactful. When tax rates change – as they inevitably will – they are unlikely to affect stocks and bonds equally. Such changes can be either good or bad. For example, eliminating or deferring the tax on reinvested dividends would be a big beneficial change for US taxable investors today (it's the case today in many other countries, but not the US).

On the other hand, an increase in capital gains tax would hurt the relative attractiveness of equities. One mitigant to this danger is your ability to choose when to realize capital gains. In a low turnover equity portfolio, by and large you're in charge of the timing, and you may be able to wait until lower capital gains rates are again reinstated years or even decades in the future. ETFs also possess certain characteristics so that, with well-managed higher turnover, the taxable investor may be able to remain in charge of realized capital gains timing.[8]

Another danger for long-term equity investors is that the world could change in a fundamental way that causes equities to go down in value and to stay down. In the last 100 years the world has suffered through two world wars, depressions, the risk of nuclear wars, disease epidemics, and other calamities. Yet economies and equity values historically have had a way of rebounding after the dark times and the world overall is more prosperous than ever. Certainly, the world is full of risk, but human ingenuity and our fundamental optimism, not to mention survival instinct, have brought our global economy and many individual countries through challenging times. I expect that trend to persist.[9]

---

[8]ETFs can trade essentially by swapping securities instead of selling them in a way that no net capital gains are realized. In fact, some ETF managers sell stocks that lock in realized losses and swap stocks with unrealized gains to avoid triggering a taxable gain. Whether this tax advantage, created in Nixon-era tax law, will be allowed to remain is an open question, so check before you buy.

[9]My perspective on time horizon is not without debate. On the one hand, I find Jeremy Siegel's work on securities prices – including his influential book *Stocks for the Long Run* – that explain the benefits of long-term equity ownership and long-time horizon compelling. On the other hand, Nobel Prize winners Paul A. Samuelson, Robert C. Merton, and others argued that a longer horizon does not improve the risk characteristics of stocks. The Vanguard Group sponsored an excellent summary of various viewpoints called "Time Diversification and Horizon-Based Asset Allocations," written by Donald G. Bennyhoff in 2008. After a thorough discussion he concludes, "Indeed, the investment horizon is considered by leading investment and financial planning professional associations to be a key factor in developing investment policy statements and asset allocations."

KEY CHAPTER TAKEAWAYS

- Measured using a long time horizon, stocks become much less risky relative to bonds. The impact of taxation on standard deviation has not been fully explored but does not appear to change these conclusions.
- Most taxable investors can and should use a long time horizon.
- In the short run the stock market is a voting machine, not a weighing machine. Focus on the fundamentals, recognize the dangers, and stay the course.

CHAPTER SIX

Control Cash Flow to Perpetuate Purchasing Power

Spending less or saving more adds resilience and power to your personal financial picture. In Chapter 4, you observed the power of compounding. In Figure 4.1, you saw that stocks grew a hundred times or more than bonds on an after-tax basis, over a simulated 30-year period. In Figure 4.2, you noticed how consistent the long-term outperformance of stocks has been and how much more stable equity returns became as you moved from 5-year to 20-year rolling measurement periods. Both these charts were cash flow neutral, which, in reality, almost no one is. Cash flow is a major risk factor. It adds to or undercuts the power of compounding, especially in the face of the notorious shorter-term volatility of stocks.

You may have heard the story of the six-foot-tall cowboy who drowned trying to ford a river that was, on average, three feet deep. The average may have been three feet, but midstream, where the current ran fastest, the depth was seven feet and the cowboy couldn't swim. Start to finish averages, like those explored in Chapter 4, are only useful if we can get across the river. In our world of taxable investing, the biggest factor that impacts whether we get across the proverbial river is cash flow. Having to sell assets to fund a 4%, 5%, or higher spending rate when your portfolio is suffering amidst a bear market can be devastating, especially if you have to pay capital gains tax to support your spending. In contrast, being able to invest dollars through a market cycle, including near the bottom, sets you powerfully for a rebound.

Cash flow strategy is a key component of managing taxable wealth. Adding regularly to your investments or, conversely, spending from them – or paying capital gains taxes now versus far in the future – have big additional impacts, positive or negative, on long-term compounding, wealth creation, and ultimately on purchasing power. Fortunately, cash flow into or out of your investment portfolio is one of the few aspects of a wealth management plan over which you have considerable control.

In the current investment return environment, taxable investors are not likely to maintain their purchasing power and their wealth over time if they spend more than 2% after tax, or $20,000 on each $1 million of assets.[1] In a highly tax-efficient portfolio the spending rate could be a bit higher; in a portfolio that generates short-term taxable gains or current income the number is lower.

Spending less or regularly saving money through market cycles adds to the power of equity compounding. It also reduces risk, especially when stock markets are performing poorly. You can't control market volatility or government tax rates, but you can diffuse their impact on your investment program. If you add to your investments in good times and bad, you're regularly adding to your asset base, even if market fluctuations cause your portfolio's value to bounce around. Sometimes you're adding at highly attractive valuations; sometimes they are less so. But, as you saw previously,

---

[1] My previous book, *Wealth: Grow It and Protect It* (FT Press, 2013), devotes an entire chapter to studying the intersection of long-term growth goals, investment returns, and leakages: spending, taxes, costs, and inflation. In summary, it is hard to grow and spend wealth.

in the long term, equity values have risen and, consequentially, so would the value of each new dollar added to your portfolio. Particularly during extended market downturns, it's enormously beneficial not to further deplete assets through spending; simply put, you will be better off if you have more capital, invested at lower valuations, to participate in an eventual upturn.

Being a regular saver and adding to your equity investments both in good times and in times of stress is an especially important concept for people in early and mid-career. Investing even $5,000 or $10,000 a year can cause your financial assets to grow into millions and millions of dollars over a 50-year career, setting you up for a comfortable retirement and more.

Here's an additional consideration. If you can add to your investments, you've planned not to be dependent on them for current spending. You are more financially resilient because you have career and/or business assets, and personal financial assets at your disposal. If one is jeopardized the other is there, just in case. This situation may not last a lifetime (though I know numerous people who enjoy working well into their 80s), but it can last an entire career, time enough to build that large nest egg. In addition, the longer we earn income, the less reliant we are on our savings, and the less risky our personal financial profile.

Once you begin drawing on financial assets for spending, in retirement or otherwise, you are in a particularly strong position to withstand the ups and downs of markets if your financial plan includes a spending rate that is the same as or lower than the annual dividend and coupon payments from your investment portfolio. In the last 70-plus years, dividend payments have been much more resilient than equity prices during economic downturns. Since World War II ended, the US stock market has experienced 29 corrections (between 10% and 20% decline) plus 11 bear markets (20% or greater decline). Three of those declines approached 50% or more.[2] In contrast, rolling annual dividend

[2] Yardeni Research, "Stock Market Briefing: S&P500 Bull & Bear Market Tables," February 13, 2018, p. 4.

payments declined more than 5% only four times and only once, during the financial crisis of 2007–9, did they fall double digits.[3]

Since there have been 40 important stock market declines in the last 73 years and only four (or arguably one) important dividend declines over the same period, I encourage you to focus on dividend volatility during stock market swoons to help you moderate the real and emotional impact of stock market declines.[4] If you are, or were, a business owner, I would wager that you mostly focused on business fundamentals rather than some notional value of your company. Now that you have more financial assets, I encourage you to keep your long-term fundamental focus and pay only limited attention to market volatility, except as a possible buying opportunity.

If your cash requirements from your investments can be satisfied solely by spending dividends, you give your plan and portfolio

3

Peak Dividend Month (rolling 12-month data)	Trough Dividend Month (rolling 12-month data)	Dividend % Decline	Months to Recover Previous Peak
September 2008	March 2010	24.1%	47
March 2000	June 2001	6.4%	43
September 1956	February 1957	6.0%	40
June 1951	December 1952	9.6%	45

Source: Wealth Strategist Partners and stock market data used in *Irrational Exuberance,* by Robert J. Shiller (Princeton University Press, 2000, 2005, 2015); data updated through 2018, http://www.econ.yale.edu/~shiller/data.htm.

[4]In the 80 years before World War II ended the picture of stock dividend volatility and relative distributions from stocks and bonds was quite different. Dividend yields were much higher, much more volatile, and slower to recover after a downturn. Dividend yields were also consistently higher than bond yields. That data series would lead someone to different conclusions about the reliability and recovery of dividend payments. A lot has changed that has led me to the conclusion to cautiously set the data from that earlier period aside. Companies are more global, they are highly responsive to changing economic circumstances, corporate governance is better, and they have many more options to finance their balance sheets. These and other improvements in recent decades give me more confidence that dividends are likely to remain relatively predictable and stable into the future. But history shows that outcome is not assured.

additional fortitude and resilience. Mature, tax-efficient portfolios are likely to have unrealized capital gains even in market downturns. If you're just spending dividend income, you won't to have to sell stock and pay capital gains tax in order to meet your spending needs. You also won't have to sell stocks to meet obligations at depressed levels, when they are cheapest. In addition, long-term equity appreciation drives growth of dividends, giving you more to spend in the long run.

If you're in the fortuitous position not to need even the dividends that a portfolio generates, you may be tempted to tilt your stocks toward lower dividend-paying stocks. If this could be done without sacrificing performance, there could be significant tax savings because a greater proportion of total returns could be in the form of deferable long-term capital gains. Even though the dividend tax rate is essentially the same today as it is for long-term gains, taxes need to be paid every year. Lower dividends *could* mean fewer taxes.

Unfortunately, the actual evidence doesn't support the logical conclusion. There appears to be a structural tradeoff between avoiding high-dividend-paying stocks and maintaining performance on a pretax basis. Academic study suggests this inefficiency is roughly the same size as the tax benefit that could accrue assuming current federal tax rates.[5] The pattern recognition that comes from my practical experience reinforces the research. On the other hand, in high-tax states the balance of tradeoffs changes and may increase the efficacy of a reduced dividend strategy; and if we return to a tax code that once again taxes dividends at income tax rates, not capital gains rates, it would definitely be worth reassessing the benefits of a reduced dividend strategy.

I have not found academic literature to confirm or undermine this next conclusion, but practical experience has suggested that a modest overweight to dividends may not adversely affect pretax performance. For taxable investors who want to spend no more than their dividends so they don't have to sell in bear markets, but seek to spend more than the market index offers, it may be possible

[5]Ronen Israel, Joseph Liberman, Nathan Sosner, and Lixin Wang, "Should Taxable Investors Shun Dividends?" *Journal of Wealth Management*, August 26, 2019.

to "tilt" an indexed portfolio to generate a little more dividend income than the market yield. Yes, the taxes will be a little higher but that may be a price worth paying for more peace of mind and a little more cash flow.

As wealth accumulates, whether they spend a small proportion of financial assets or a larger percentage. many people redeploy some amount of their financial assets into personal assets. When considering buying a second home, a nicer car, collectibles, or a new sailboat, think about the financial implications. One family office executive I really respect coined the "3%/6% Rule": converting a $100,000 financial asset that generates 3% of income or dividends into a personal asset that costs 6% a year to maintain is a decision that creates a 9% negative swing in cash flow. In order to fill the gap, you may need to sell additional financial assets each year to fund your additional costs. If that $100,000 financial asset or any subsequent sales have low cost basis, the tax bill further adds to the "cost" of converting financial into personal assets. Your numbers will vary, but when you make an important decision like this, your analysis should consider all these factors. I'm not saying, "Don't do it," but I encourage you to do your homework. Building a cushion of wealth gives us the capacity to take control of our financial affairs rather than them dictating to us. An important factor in building that cushion is managing the relationship between our assets and our spending.

KEY CHAPTER TAKEAWAYS

- Spending less or regularly saving more through market cycles adds to the power of compounding and asymmetry of compounding return; in short, spending less reduces risk.
- If you spend no more than your dividends, you never have to sell and pay capital gains tax to meet those spending requirements.

CHAPTER SEVEN

Don't Be Misled by Performance

Business leaders rely on Key Performance Indicators (KPIs) to keep tabs on their enterprises. Taxable investors should do the same. But too often, the metrics used by taxable investors, if they are used at all, are flawed. The investment industry standard for measuring managers of liquid investment portfolios of stocks, bonds, and other publicly traded securities – including hedge funds – is the Time-Weighted Rate of return (TWR); for private investment portfolios like leveraged buyout, venture capital, and real estate funds, the standard is pretax Internal Rate of Return (IRR).[1] Such measures may be fine for tax-exempt institutional investors, but for us taxable investors, these are necessary but insufficient. Even though they are the industry standard KPIs, neither captures the impact of taxes.

---

[1] TWRs measure returns independent of cash flow. In other words, they measure the growth of a dollar invested at the beginning of a time period, throughout that time period. It assumes no additional cash flows in or out. IRRs incorporate the timing of cash flow into the return calculation. Both TWRs and IRRs are typically (but not always) presented as annualized figures. For more detailed explanation, visit www .investopedia.com.

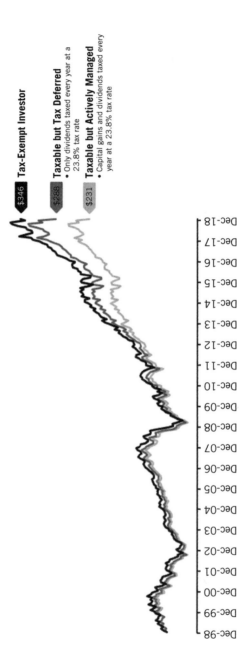

FIGURE 7.1 GROWTH OF $100², JANUARY 1, 1999, TO December 31, 2018.

Tax-Exempt Investor

Taxable but Tax Deferred
• Only dividends taxed every year at a 23.8% tax rate

Taxable but Actively Managed
• Capital gains and dividends taxed every year at a 23.8% tax rate

$346
$288
$231

Dec-98 Dec-99 Dec-00 Dec-01 Dec-02 Dec-03 Dec-04 Dec-05 Dec-06 Dec-07 Dec-08 Dec-09 Dec-10 Dec-11 Dec-12 Dec-13 Dec-14 Dec-15 Dec-16 Dec-17 Dec-18

[2]Source: Wealth Strategist Partners analysis using Morningstar, Inc. data for the Vanguard 500 Index Fund Investor Shares. ©2020 Morningstar, Inc. All Rights Reserved. Reproduced with permission.

Figure 7.1 shows the dollar growth of three portfolios of publicly traded equities with identical TWRs, but with different investors and different tax profiles.

The top track record in black shows the dollar return for a tax-exempt investor, who is indifferent to whether profits come in the form of income, dividends, short-term, or long-term capital gains. The light and dark gray track records are for taxable investors. The dark gray track record is for a portfolio managed so that the portfolio's dividends are taxed each year and the net is reinvested. The net capital gains remain unrealized throughout the 20 years and accrue untaxed. This is what a well-managed index fund or ETF can do. The light gray track record is for a portfolio managed so that all net capital gains are realized each year as long-term capital gains only. Turnover is effectively 100%, taxes are paid each year on dividends and capital gains, and the net after-tax profits are reinvested.[3] To repeat, the TWRs as measured by standard industry practice are exactly the same for the three portfolios, but the outcomes for each investor vary substantially. The impact of an investor's tax status and of manager investment decisions affecting the tax efficiency of their portfolios isn't captured in TWRs.[4]

To take an extreme example of the impact of investment decisions on taxes, let's examine the situation where two different managers buy the same stock on the same day for $100. One manager holds the stock for 364 days before selling at $200; the other manager holds for two more days and also sells for $200. Simply because one manager sells right before the stock

---

[3] It's true that 100% turnover is above some measures of average active mutual fund turnover, which could be interpreted to penalize active management. To counterbalance, the model assumes no taxation at the higher short-term rates. In addition, the effect of taxation and turnover on the power of compounding is minimal until taxable turnover drops below 10 to 15%, approaching the realm of low-turnover index funds. Looked at a different way, until average holding periods in a portfolio of stocks approach 10 years or more, the difference between holding stocks a year and a day versus two years, or five years, is minimal.

[4] Many managers will show their performance using a similar "growth of a dollar chart." Just remember that these charts are accurate for tax-exempt investors only. You need to dig deeper to understand the true growth of your dollars. Mutual funds must report in their prospectuses an estimate of after-tax dollars. No other investment managers are required to do so.

becomes subject to long-term capital gains tax and the other waits two days, the difference to a taxable investor in net after-tax value is $17 or 17% of the profit. (If you annualize that 17% differential created over two days, it's a big, big number.) Again, those manager actions don't get captured into performance calculations, but they do in your pocketbook.

Investment managers' decisions complicate your financial life in other ways. Since they don't pay your taxes from their portfolios you must find the money from somewhere else, or you have to withdraw it proactively from each manager to pay the taxes their decisions cause. Mutual funds and ETFs must distribute net income and net realized gains to investors late each calendar year, in ample time for you to set aside a portion to pay tax. You may automatically reinvest the pretax distributed gains or receive them in cash. Either way they are taxable. Some hedge funds don't even file K-1 tax filings in time to meet your April 15 tax deadline, and they don't automatically distribute their gains. If you don't proactively withdraw the tax triggered by each hedge fund from that fund, you must come up with the tax payment from other sources. The net effect is that you are adding money to the hedge funds that generate your highest tax bills. Is that what you intend?

Although TWRs are flawed for taxable investors, it is still useful to measure the TWRs of each manager as one measure of *their* performance. It's equally important to measure the TWR of all your managers and your other investments together – your total portfolio. This aggregate measure of performance aims to capture the quality of *your* manager selection decisions and the effectiveness of *your* capital allocation decisions among them. Choosing good managers is important, but so are the decisions about when to give them assets to manage, when to remove assets from them, and how much to give them. These decisions get captured, at least to some extent, in your aggregate performance data. Aggregate performance helps to hold your financial advisor and yourself accountable.

A good way to help assess aggregate performance is to benchmark it. You can compare your aggregate portfolio TWR to the TWR of a blended benchmark of investable indexes that mirrors the risk of your portfolio. A comparison of annualized percentage returns is typically made over multiple time periods, ranging out to 10 years or more. If, over most periods, your actual performance meets or exceeds the benchmark, that is generally deemed to be good. But determining the right benchmark(s) and interpreting the comparative results for your portfolio range from science to an art form, depending on the complexity of your investment program.

If you own only a few broad market index funds and you have a target weighting for each, your benchmark should be a blend of the indexes you've chosen to mimic, weighted by the target weighting. Your actual portfolio's performance should track the benchmark's performance very closely. That's pretty scientific. In this case, both your portfolio of indexes and the benchmark of indexes will have only small amounts of turnover caused either by the sale of companies within each index or turnover associated with infrequent rebalancing. Therefore, they are likely to be highly tax-efficient, especially when the equity component is a large percentage of the total.

Benchmarking more complex – and, often, less tax-efficient – portfolios adds to the art. Start with a "static benchmark" that has a fixed weighting among stocks, bonds, and cash. The previous paragraph described such a static benchmark. As one way we measure performance, my clients use a static benchmark of between 70% and 80% the MSCI All Country World Equity Index and 20% to 30% the Barclay's Aggregate Bond Index. (As taxable investors, one could arguably use a municipal bond index to replace the Barclay's Aggregate, which uses taxable bonds. One could add a cash component to the benchmark, too.) The more aggressive your portfolio, the higher the equity component should be. But I recommend 80% equities as an upper bound. Even in aggressive portfolios, you want to signal some benefit to diversification.

It's unlikely your actual portfolio, whether simple or highly complex, will be more tax-efficient than the static benchmark, so it should at least approach the benchmark's performance on a pretax basis. If you're going to add complexity to your investment strategy you should want, at very least, to measure whether it's adding value relative to the simple, tax-efficient approach represented by the static benchmark. You will also get early signals if your portfolio isn't performing up to par, so long as you artfully and scientifically interpret the results.

Another percentage-based benchmark that some investors use is an "active benchmark." The weightings in this type of benchmark mirror the actual weightings of the asset classes in the portfolio it is benchmarking. That is simple enough. The tricky part is figuring out which benchmark components to use, especially for alternative investments, and then interpreting the results. It's also feasible to compare a portfolio's performance to a that of a universe of other investors. I don't put as much credence in this benchmark because objectives and strategies vary considerably, but it can reasonably be part of a broader mosaic.

Percentage-based return measures, in addition to providing incomplete information for taxable investors, are not intuitive for many people. Dollars are intuitive for just about everyone. Plus, you can't spend percentages. It's valuable to track the dollar value of portfolios over time net of all leakages: fees, taxes, inflation and spending/contributions. The dollar value should also be tracked over time relative to the portfolio's aggregate cost basis. With this information you can answer these important questions: Is my portfolio growing in real terms? Is it growing because of cash flow or because of investment performance net of fees and taxes? If you also track your portfolio's ratio of cost to market value and the amount of deferred tax, you will see how tax efficiency varies with time and market performance. This also is a reminder to think about the costs of selling appreciated securities and the income and growth generated by their deferred taxes.

Just as you benchmark your total portfolio, you can benchmark the performance of each manager. A manager investing in public markets will typically tell you which index they are trying to meet or beat, measured using TWRs. If they don't, then ask. You should be the judge of whether the benchmark is appropriate, but most of the time it will be. You can measure each manager's results relative to the agreed benchmark as an important indicator of their performance. Again, the more complex the manager's strategy, the more likely their performance will diverge significantly from the benchmark and the greater the scope for (mis)interpretation of results.

In private market investing like private equity and venture capital funds, TWRs are an inappropriate metric for measuring returns. Pretax internal rate of return (IRR) is the right numeric measure of performance. This is because when you invest in public markets, you determine when to give more money to a manager, or when to take it away. In private markets investing, once you have committed to a fund, it's the manager that decides when to draw and when to return your capital. The quality of those timing decisions is not captured in TWRs, but it is using IRRs.

Unfortunately, IRRs don't do any better job at capturing tax efficiency than TWRs. A high-turnover private investment fund with a double-digit IRR may be a less good investment for a taxable investor than one with a high single-digit IRR and lower turnover. But the decisions and incentives of most institutional investors are driven by IRRs, and institutional investors are by far the biggest consumers of private markets investment funds. This phenomenon is driving private investment funds away from a long-term perspective, to the detriment of taxable investors. That's why in addition to IRRs, I recommend that you track three other measures of performance: 1) the Multiple Of Invested Capital (MOIC) – if you invested a dollar, how much is it now worth?; 2) the public market equivalent – if you invested the same money in similar public markets would you have done better or worse?; and 3) a measure of relative performance by vintage year and asset class – how did the manager do relative to its competition? Together, especially measured over the life of each fund's investment, these four measures give you a good numerical dashboard.

Whether you're investing in public or private markets, you can use year-end tax forms – including 1099s and K-1s – to collect information on the tax efficiency of each manager. You can use this data to estimate and compare the pretax and after-tax profitability of each manager. If you ask, most managers will say they are tax conscious. Doing this work, or asking your accountant to do so, will demonstrate how true the assertion is. But you may have to push. I recently gave a speech at the annual meeting of an accounting firm proposing this as a great way to add value to their private clients' investment process. Someone came up to me after and explained that doing so could upset their hedge fund clients. I guess they earn more doing accounting work for hedge funds than for hedge fund investors. On the other hand, members of the research team from the well-known hedge fund firm AQR recently published a methodology for measuring the after-tax performance of hedge funds.[5]

In conclusion, there is no perfect measure of after-tax returns, but you shouldn't abandon your instincts to insist upon developing and using KPIs to measure the performance of your financial assets. I suspect that the KPIs you use in business aren't perfect either. They need continuous refinement and knowing interpretation. Remember that even imperfect measures of performance can improve your understanding and help you make better decisions. Plus, the weaker your measurement system, the greater the opportunity to make big mistakes and not realize their impact until too late.

KEY CHAPTER TAKEAWAYS

- Develop an accountability system that measures the long-term performance of your total portfolio and each of your managers. Track your portfolio growth in dollars as well as in percentages.
- Use the conventional metrics but understand their limitations for a taxable portfolio. Neither IRRs nor TWRs measure how well managers' decisions affect after-tax performance; therefore, they can be misleading. Managers with similar performance measured by TWRs or IRRs can generate very different results regarding what actually ends up in your pocket.

[5] Nathan Sosner, Rodney Sullivan, and Liliana Urrutia's article titled "Multi-Period After-Tax Reporting: A Practical Solution," in the *Journal of Wealth Management* 21 (no. 3, Winter 2018) describes a methodology for after-tax reporting of hedge funds. If hedge fund managers, private equity managers, or separate account managers don't provide after-tax reporting, ask them to provide you data from the Form K-1 from a long-term investor and do your own analysis of tax impact.

- Regularly calculate (or have your accountant calculate) and compare the pretax and after-tax performance of each of your managers. It will change the way you invest and whom you hire to manage assets on your behalf.
- Track the inflation-adjusted performance of your portfolio in dollars, net of friction costs, to determine if it's actually growing.

CHAPTER EIGHT

Get Value from Active Management

As we were reminded early in Chapter 4, over the long run, the odds are low of beating the market through active management of public equities, even before tax considerations. Nevertheless, it seems part of the human psyche that hope springs eternal that a smart manager can buy and sell stocks on a timely basis to generate above average returns.

Some active managers trade second to second; others may hold investments for years. Either way, after-tax success in active management is made harder by the fact that such activity creates tax drag. In fact, the very search for outperformance makes active management less efficient in taxable portfolios.

A colleague and I have done a detailed study asking this question: "How much value does an active equity manager need to generate just to match the performance of a broad-based index, net of tax?" The answer is that a manager must add an average of 1.5% to 2.5% of incremental performance above the index each year over two decades just to match the performance of their indexed benchmark. And that assumes the manager's net realized gains are all taxed at the lower long-term capital gains rate. We then studied the Morningstar database of active mutual funds to determine the likelihood of an active manager generating that much extra benefit. Based on history, the odds that any one actively managed mutual fund will match the performance of a comparable index fund over a 20-year time frame, net of tax – let alone do better – are only between 5% and 20%, depending on market conditions.[1] The odds of performing materially better than the index are even lower. Robert Jeffrey, who did pioneering analytical work on taxable investing, grouped the performance of funds that outperformed the S&P 500 after tax and, separately, those that underperformed. He concluded, "My math is pretty simplistic, but I'm not thrilled with the odds of a bet on which I have a 14% chance of picking up 130 basis points of return and an 86% chance of losing 320."[2] Magnitude and probability speak for themselves. Fortunately, later in the chapter I will discuss some things you can do to improve the situation.

But first, I have more bad news: additional factors worsen the odds of success. More often than not, replacing an active equity manager – for any reason – is likely to trigger capital gains taxes. Newly hired managers tend to disavow their predecessors' decisions and want to start with a clean slate. So, they sell the previously owned portfolio. Since most of the time, equity portfolios rise in value and most active managers defer at least some gains year over year, legacy portfolios inevitably build net deferred tax liabilities. This is true whether the manager has performed well or poorly relative to its benchmark. When a

---

[1] Stuart Lucas and Alejandro Sanz, "Pick Your Battles: The Intersection of Investment Strategy, Tax, and Compounding Returns," *Journal of Wealth Management* 19 (no. 2, Fall 2016). In the reference section of the article you will find citations of other academic studies that corroborate our findings.

[2] Robert H. Jeffrey, "Tax-Efficient Investing Is Easier Said Than Done," *Journal of Wealth Management*, Summer 2001. This article was written as a reply to "How Well Have Taxable Investors Been Served in the 1980s and 1990s?" by Robert D. Arnott, Andrew L. Berkin, PhD, and Jia Ye, CFA, in the *Journal of Portfolio Management*. This is a broader, deeper analysis of "Is Your Alpha Big Enough to Cover Your Taxes," by Arnott and Jeffrey in 1993 in the same journal. Subsequently this article has been revisited by Arnott, Berkin, and Paul Bouchey, CFA, and most recently in 2018 by Arnott alone through the firm Research Affiliates, as a 25-year retrospective.

manager gets replaced the tax payments are triggered, diminishing the net after-tax investable assets available to reinvest.[3] Through time and performance, the more the legacy portfolio has built deferred tax liabilities, the larger the potential tax obligation triggered by replacing the manager. This phenomenon further lowers your odds of success. It is a hidden cost that few taxable investors consider when setting investment strategy.

I call it *the cost of being wrong* because these actions are most often associated with changing a manager who has underperformed expectations. But it's also a cost if you trim a successful investment to rebalance your portfolio, or if you selected a successful manager who, a decade or two later, retires without a compelling succession plan.

There's a further problem. Most people don't have just one active manager of public equities. Every active manager in your portfolio must outperform by 1.5% to 2.5% for your overall portfolio to match the market net of tax. If even one manager doesn't achieve that level of outperformance it places an even greater burden on all the others to perform even better, further lowering the odds of overall success. Compounding poor odds, on top of poor odds, on top of poor odds, is not a recipe for success.

Nevertheless, the allure of superior profits, not to mention the lure of the enticing marketing spend of active managers and their distributors, drive many people to active management. "I just hate the thought of being average" is a common retort.

TACTICS FOR IMPROVING SUCCESS WITH ACTIVE MANAGERS

This does not mean that no one can ever beat the market. It just means that you need to be very conscious of whether you are getting

---

[3] Wealthier investors can structure their manager relationships through "separate accounts," though check that the cost is reasonable. Separate accounts offer the opportunity to switch managers without having to sell the entire portfolio. This can substantially reduce "the cost of being wrong" if the new manager doesn't simply sell everything to start fresh. This is not an option for mutual fund investors or all but the largest ETF investors.

outperformance from an active manager net of fees and tax. If you are determined to invest in actively managed portfolios, there are things you can do to improve the odds of success. First, although it may sound obvious, to achieve sufficient outperformance to add value net of fees and tax, actively managed portfolios can't look much like the index. In other words, they need "high tracking error." Tracking error is a measure of how different a portfolio's holdings are from the holdings in the benchmark it is trying to beat. A high-tracking-error manager's performance diverges more from the index than a low-tracking-error manager's, both to the upside and to the downside. Higher divergence can amplify the pain of underperformance, but at least it creates some chance of success.

Taxable investors could really use a robust academic study that evaluates the chance of low-tracking-error equity portfolios actually meeting or exceeding the 1.5% to 2.5% hurdle rate over the index. Figure 8.1 shows how I anticipate a chart of the results would appear.

I predict that such a study would confirm that low-tracking-error, actively managed, equity portfolios are almost destined to

FIGURE **8.1**   CONCEPTUAL FRAMEWORK OF THE RELATIONSHIP BETWEEN TRACKING ERROR AND VALUE ADDED.

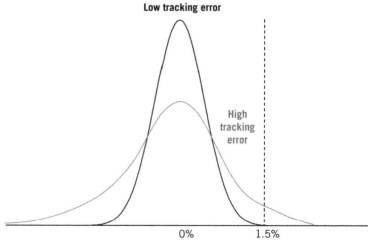

Low tracking error

High tracking error

0%   1.5%

Value Added Over Benchmark

fall short after fees and taxes and, as a result, are a bad deal for taxable investors. A colleague and I tested this thesis by analyzing the Morningstar equity mutual fund database. Of all the funds that exceeded a 1.5% annualized excess return, only 5% had tracking error below 4%. Looked at another way, the odds of those lower-tracking-error funds exceeding the 1.5% threshold were less than 1% and that is before considering the funds tax efficiency.[4]

Another potential benefit of higher-tracking-error funds is that there is some evidence to suggest that high-tracking-error equity mutual funds may have experienced modestly better performance on average than low-tracking-error mutual funds, but the evidence is hardly overwhelming.[5]

If you are going to invest in actively managed portfolios of publicly traded equities, I recommend a simple screening process to build a group of potentially attractive active managers for taxable portfolios. From the universe of active managers, first, eliminate those strategies and funds with less than 4% tracking error. Indexing will generate better net long-term results and lower fees, with a high degree of certainty.

Second, from the group that passes the first screen, eliminate those managers with turnover that exceeds 50% per year, especially when the turnover produces a preponderance of short-term capital gains that are taxed at a higher rate than long-term capital gains.[6] It's hard enough to beat a 1.5% alpha hurdle rate with

[4]My colleague Alejandro Sanz and I analyzed the Morningstar equity mutual fund database from 4/1/2009 to 3/31/2019. We used 5-year rolling tracking errors in this analysis. This time period was not an ideal sample, but it is a start. It is a relatively short time period and it was a period when the stock market largely went in one direction: up. I hope that curious academics will collect the data and do more robust analyses in the future to help taxable investors and their advisors understand better when active management might make sense.

[5]K.J. Martijn Cremers, Jon A. Fulkerson, and Timothy B. Riley, "Challenging the Conventional Wisdom on Active Management: A Review of the Past 20 Years of Academic Literature on Actively Managed Mutual Funds," *Financial Analysts Journal* 75 (no. 4, 2019), pp. 12–13.

[6]Mutual funds prospectuses must show the short-term capital gains distributions and long-term capital gains distributions made each year. This will indicate not only how much capital gain they realize it will also show the proportion of short-and long-term gains.

FIGURE 8.2   SCREENING MATRIX FOR TAXABLE EQUITY MANAGERS.

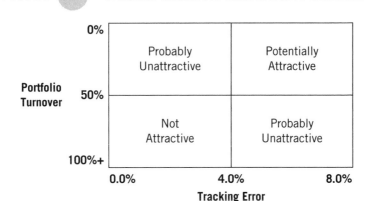

relatively low turnover. As turnover and tax inefficiency rise, so should the hurdle rate, recognizing that it will be harder and harder for the manager to add value net of tax.

Visually, you can think of the screen as a 2-by-2 matrix, as seen in Figure 8.2. In the upper right-hand quadrant, you will be left with a group of potentially attractive managers, but these same managers are more likely to have periods of significant underperformance.

That is why I would add a third screen. Eliminate any remaining funds and strategies where the manager doesn't have a substantial personal investment alongside your own. I sleep better when my managers' own capital benefits from good performance and suffers real economic impact from weak performance.

Management fees are a first claim on client assets, regardless of performance. Profit participations (carried interest) are a claim on profit but not on losses. They are both asymmetric incentives – heads I win, tails you lose – and don't help with my sleep. Only when a manager has a significant personal financial stake alongside my own is the symmetry and alignment of interests closer. Then we are partners in the outcome of his or her investment decisions. This is no guarantee of superior performance, but it is a step in the right direction. When the stakes are high because tracking error is also high, this third screen is particularly important.[7]

Why is this alignment of incentives so important? Every high-tracking-error manager with a long track record goes through extended periods of underperformance. On December 22, 2016, Jeffrey Ptak, Global Director of Manager Research at Morningstar, Inc., published some research that concluded, "Long-term out-performers suffer large drawdowns just like losing funds and frequently lag their indexes over the short term, *sometimes by dreadfully large margins* [italics added for emphasis]."[8] During those dry spells – which can last for years – I gain some comfort that

[7]Morningstar, Inc., has done some analysis over the years on mutual fund performance relative to the managers' stakes in their own funds. I would characterize the results as directionally comforting, but not conclusive. For one thing, the analyses I've reviewed don't account for tracking error. One clear conclusion is that most managers don't have very much of their net worth invested in their own funds, which is too bad. Fortunately, there are exceptions. I am aware of two investment management firms that require employees to invest 100% of their equity assets in their own products. This rare, but terrific, policy creates great alignment of interest. A few other firms have similar policies, but they are hard to find. There isn't a database that tracks the level of mutual fund manager investment above a $1 million investment, which, frankly, isn't a very big commitment. Most active mutual funds with assets over a few hundred million have annual management fees that are a multiple of this figure. I know some alternative investment managers that have hundreds of millions of dollars, or more, invested in their own funds. It is a factor in our investment due diligence process. Unfortunately, tracking down the data is difficult. The alignment of a manager's personal investments with our clients' investments provides some comfort, but I also find it useful to think about the combined effects of the manager's personal investment appreciation plus the fees and carried interest that they earn. Sometimes, even with large dollars invested, the management fee and carry are more powerful motivators.

[8]Jeffrey Ptak, CFA, "Winning Funds Often Look Like Losers: Winning funds often look more like Jay Cutler than Tom Brady," December 22, 2016. From the same article is another telling quote: "investors in these [top decile] funds spend roughly a third of the past two decades looking up, not down at the index." There are other studies of the interim performance of long-term top performers. All that I've seen draw similar conclusions; virtually every long-term top-performing manager goes through years when performance relative to their chosen index is poor. Here are a couple of additional citations: "The Truth About Top-Performing Money Managers: Why investors should expect – and accept – periods of poor relative performance"

the manager and I are sharing the pain and that he or she is doing his or her best to persist through times when the manager's strategy is not in synch with market sentiment. That alignment of interest helps me to hang in there.

It also helps to be timely and then be prepared to stay the course – or invest more – especially through periods of weak relative performance and to hope that the tide turns before your patience runs out.

Some investors will choose an alternate path – selecting the stocks of individual companies that they think will be great long-term performers and then holding those stocks for really long periods. The upside of holding a select basket of individual securities for a long time is that the typical 1.5% to 2.5% hurdle rate to beat the market after tax drops toward zero. This strategy could have no turnover. Or, if there is turnover, it could be a function of companies in your portfolio being acquired, typically at a premium to the market that's large enough to cover the tax bill.

If you consider going this challenging but potentially rewarding path, take a look at Figure 8.3. This chart shows a list of the top-10-performing companies in the S&P 500 over the last 20 years, ending September 30, 2019; though you could choose any 20-year period and the patterns would be similar.

First, ask yourself, "How many of these top-performing companies have I ever heard of?" Sure, you know Apple and you may drink Monster beverages. If you're in the tech world you probably know NVIDIA and if you're in biotech you know Celgene. But how about HollyFrontier, Cognizant, Tractor Supply, or NVR? Would you have identified any of these 20 years ago, invested in them, and held on? Most weren't even in the S&P 500 20 years ago even though they were all public. Other of today's high-profile stocks weren't public 20 years ago. If you had bought Netflix after its IPO you would have done fantastically well, up over 240 times. On the other hand, stocks like Facebook, Amazon, or

F I G U R E   **8.3**   **S&P 500's Top 20-Year Performers.**

Security	Annualized Total Return	Multiple of Initial Price	Maximum Drawdown		
			Magnitude	Start	End
Monster Beverage Corp	37.1%	549x	−69.2%	Oct 07	May 11
NVIDIA Corp	29.5%	176x	−89.7%	Jan 02	Mar 06
Apple Inc	27.0%	118x	−81.8%	Mar 00	Jan 05
HollyFrontier Corp	26.5%	110x	−86.0%	Jul 07	Jul 11
Cognizant Technology Solutions Corp A	25.5%	93x	−71.3%	Mar 00	Nov 02
Ansys Inc	25.2%	89x	−63.3%	Jun 08	Nov 10
Celgene Corp	25.1%	87x	−84.6%	Sep 00	Apr 05
Tractor Supply Co	24.8%	83x	−67.4%	Apr 00	Jul 01
NVR Inc	24.0%	73x	−65.9%	Jul 05	Dec 12
IDEXX Laboratories Inc.	23.0%	62x	−57.3%	Nov 07	Apr 10

Source: Based on data from ©2020 Morningstar, Inc.

Alphabet (Google), have only compounded at a fraction of the same rate as public companies.

The top performers of the next 20 years are unlikely to be well known or understood today. To identify them proactively takes deep research, insight, and more than a little luck. On the other hand, if you had all those things 20 years ago and identified these companies (and not too many that didn't deliver on their promise), your returns would have been fantastic.

That said, would you have stayed the course? Every single firm mentioned above experienced a multiyear drawdown of between 57% and 90% along the path to success. Would you have persisted in your ownership when a $1 investment turned into 10 cents, or would you have thrown in the towel and taken a tax loss? Even more to the point, would you have doubled your investment near the bottom? By the way, look at the dates of the drawdowns. They didn't necessarily happen during the internet bubble or the financial crisis, though admittedly there was usually overlap. In short, for those who wish to try this strategy, the research and emotional challenges are substantial.

There is an interesting intermediate path between pure indexing and pure active management – whether investing in funds or directly into stocks – that may lower the 1.5% hurdle rate and make selected lower-tracking-error funds relatively attractive. It is called "factor-based" investing. Academic study has determined that there are anomalies in financial markets that give investors better returns without taking more risk.[9] For those who believe in efficient markets, it's kind of like having your cake and eating it too. On average, factor-based portfolios that tilt toward these identified anomalies, such as value investing, smaller capitalization stocks, higher-quality stocks, and other factors, have historically outperformed. Some mutual funds have been able to do so with high levels of tax efficiency, in part because they have low structural turnover, and in part because they have attracted a lot of cash flow, which allows them to shift portfolio weightings without selling. These factors may not work over periods of a few years, but over longer periods their results have been consistently better. Nobel Prize winner Eugene Fama from the University of Chicago and Kenneth French from Dartmouth College were pioneers in the discovery and study of factor-based investing.

More and more excellent firms, large and small, promote factor-based investing. One big issue for taxable investors is to make sure that factor "tilts" don't undermine tax efficiency. For example, "value companies" sometimes become "growth companies" and no longer fit their factor model. On the one hand that is good because the transformation is usually associated with a rising stock price. On the other, selling a successful investment will create turnover and tax. Tracking error and tax efficiency in factor-based investing can vary widely from provider to provider

---

[9]There is some evidence that academic spotlights on anomalies like factor-based investing may initially reinforce the very benefits that are discovered and then, with the findings disseminated in academic journals, they become arbitraged away. For more information, refer to R. David McLean and Jeffrey Pontiff, "Does Academic Research Destroy Stock Return Predictability?" *Journal of Finance*, forthcoming.

and portfolio to portfolio. Nevertheless, there are factor-based mutual funds and ETFs that have been tax efficient. Portfolio design, the amount of cash flow coming into mutual funds that can be used to rebalance without having to sell appreciated securities, and the capacity of ETFs to manage taxes[10] are key. Suffice it to say that a well-designed factor-based portfolio with a tracking error below 4% could be a successful alternative for a taxable investor even if it doesn't exceed the 1.5% performance hurdle rate. There is another challenge though: the investor needs to maintain a long enough horizon to weather times when the factor tilts aren't working. Most recently, value investing has been going through a rough period, and people are starting to question whether the bloom is off the rose.

One way to improve the odds of success in taxable investment strategies is to structure the indexed or factor-based component of your portfolio to get more out of your active high-tracking-error managers. Specifically, tax-loss harvesting techniques designed into a separately managed index or factor-based account can help offset the tax inefficiency of active management.[11] Here's

---

[10]ETFs have the capacity to rebalance their portfolios by making distributions of securities rather than selling them within the ETF. This technique enables them to defer tax within the ETF structure to the benefit of its taxable shareholders.

[11]Tax loss harvesting is an increasingly common technique offered by some index tracking managers that enables clients to sell those stocks selling below cost and to replace them with other stocks without materially degrading the portfolio's ability to closely track the performance of the index. The algorithms used also avoid "wash sales" that negate the tax loss when the same security is bought and sold within 30 days. To be able to use the tax losses to offset against gains generated by other managers, these portfolios must be structured as separate accounts. Based on personal experience and specific client factors, I estimate a benefit of 0.4% to 1.0% per year before management fees. The benefit may not sound like a lot but after 10 or 20 years it really starts to add up – and the probability of success is very high. Over time, if new cash is not added to the portfolio, fewer and fewer stocks will have market values below their costs and the incremental opportunity to generate new tax losses to offset against realized gains from active management declines toward zero. The capacity of the portfolio to shield new losses under this circumstance declines but the tax deferral from unrealized gains can continue indefinitely. Furthermore, you can pluck out the most highly appreciated stocks from the portfolio and use them for making highly tax-efficient charitable donations. Mutual fund and ETF accounting allows tax losses generated within the vehicle to offset realized gains within the

how it works. Your index tracking or factor-based investments track their benchmarks while selling stocks that lose value and holding ones that grow in value. Periodically, the losses are realized and the proceeds are reinvested using mathematical algorithms so that the total portfolio continues to closely track the index. Those realized tax losses can then be used to offset realized gains elsewhere among your financial investments. Today, accounting rules only allow "portability" of losses in a separate account structure (not a mutual fund or ETF). Stocks with gains compound indefinitely, tax-deferred. Inevitably, over time, the tax cost of selling the index-tracking portfolio will rise. That's the bad news. The good news is that as a mature tax-managed portfolio rises in value with the market, the deferred taxes grow in size, and they are deferred for longer and longer. The value creation is consistent and high probability, but modest. So the management fees need to be low – 40 basis points or less – or else it's probably best to use a broad-based index fund or ETF instead.

Another way to improve the odds of success is to move away from public markets and into less-efficient private markets. Less-efficient markets like private equity have historically generated returns well above the average for the stock market.[12] It's always better to fish where opportunity is more plentiful. It's doubly attractive when these long-term opportunities are asymmetrically positive and tax efficient. That's what the next chapter explores in greater detail.

Finally, you have additional tools at your disposal to manage the intersection of investment, tax, and estate planning to create

vehicle, but they cannot be "exported" to act as an offset against gains generated by other investments and you can't reach into their portfolios to give away individual securities.

[12] Steven N. Kaplan, the Neubauer Family Distinguished Service Professor of Entrepreneurship and Finance at University of Chicago's Booth School of Business, has analyzed and written extensively about the performance of private equity and venture capital. He has access to the best available data and has been anointed by Mike Cembalest, JP Morgan Asset Management's investment strategist, as the patron saint of private equity research. You can go to his publications listing on the university's website for a listing of his work. I particularly recommend the paper "Private Equity Performance: What We Know" with Robert Harris and Tim Jenkinson (*Journal of Finance*, 2014).

value, and to do so with high odds of success. As we saw above, the losses generated by tax-loss harvesting can increase your flexibility to shield investment profits from tax, making it possible to rebalance portfolios, lower the cost of being wrong, and defer the tax from successfully completed investments. If you have a year when your tax rate is abnormally low, you can sell highly appreciated stock at lower tax rates. In other years, highly appreciated stocks can be donated to your favorite charity with greater advantage than cash donations. As deferred taxes increase, the value of "stepped up basis at death" grows to the benefit of your heirs.

Valuable as deferred taxes are, they bring two big risks. First, a rising tax rate will increase the size of your deferred tax liability and reduce your Owner's Equity as defined in Chapter 3; the bigger the deferred tax, the bigger the adverse impact on Owner's Equity. Second, if you need to raise funds for emergencies, or to buy a house, or go on extended holiday you will need to consider your tax bill as adding to the cash you must raise to meet that need. Alternatively, you could use the portfolio as collateral for borrowing; just keep the level of borrowing in check. The last thing you want is to receive a margin call plus a big tax bill on a portfolio of highly appreciated securities.

Large deferred taxes do increase switching costs and can become an impediment to change. It's a high-class problem, but a problem to bear in mind, nonetheless. The key is to anticipate the long-term implications of investment strategy design, prepare for uncertainty, be patient and persistent, and, in opportune moments, act decisively even if there are short-term costs.

KEY CHAPTER TAKEAWAYS

- Pair tax loss harvesting indexed or factor-based separate accounts with active managers to increase the odds of success.
- Only high-tracking-error managers have a reasonable chance of adding value net of tax.
- Don't forget the cost of being wrong in your portfolio construction analysis.
- Active management is more likely to achieve success in less efficient private markets than in more efficient public ones.

CHAPTER NINE

Approach Alternative Investments with Skill and Skepticism, or Not at All

Alternative investments were once the domain of sophisticated family offices and a few early movers in the endowment and foundation world. The know-how was concentrated in few hands, capital was limited, and returns were consistently high. The markets were inefficient, so superior skill was rewarded with much higher returns. Even middling relative results usually outperformed public markets. Today, alternative investments are no longer "alternative." Those high backward-looking returns have attracted more than $7 trillion of hedge funds, credit, private equity, venture capital, and real estate funds.[1] A whole network of intermediaries has grown up to sell

---

[1] More recent additions to the list of alternative investments include life insurance settlements and litigation financing. I've studied both and, at least as of this writing, invested in neither. Although headline rates of return were high based on IRRs, the potential to compound after tax returns in dollars were not as compelling.

these investments to just about anyone who has a few million dollars to invest.[2] Alternatives have gone mainstream.

As these pools of capital have grown, the marketplaces in which they invest have become highly competitive and less inefficient. What started as a market for private taxable wealth has been flooded by tax-exempt institutional assets. Knowledge about these markets is now widespread. Managers looking to structure funds and raise capital are driven to maximize IRRs, not net after-tax profits, because they know that's what the big money institutions are looking for and it's how their own incentive compensation is usually calculated.

The opportunity to invest in these funds is everywhere, but should you invest? The headline returns always look good. The competition among managers to have standout numbers is intense and is entirely indifferent to tax efficiency; that puts us taxable investors at a competitive disadvantage from the start. Tax-exempt investors get 100% of every dollar of profit earned. We pay 20% to 50%, or more, in taxes.[3] Therefore, we have to do a lot more analysis to turn those headline numbers into a form that is actually meaningful for us. That's before the even more challenging work of assessing strategy, talent, organizational strength, ethics, and other critical success factors needed for a manager to deliver excellent results going forward. Then, we must figure out how to access the best choices.

The only objective reason for us to invest in alternatives is to generate better risk-adjusted returns, net of all friction costs, than we could achieve in a tax-efficient, fully liquid portfolio.

---

[2]Alternative investments are less regulated than traditional mutual funds and ETFs, so the SEC applies certain investor qualifications to prevent retail investors from participating in this part of the market. To invest, one needs to be an "Accredited Investor" and often a "Qualified Purchaser." These criteria require the investor to have certain scale of assets or income, but it is not a requirement that they possess particular knowledge. In recent years, firms are creating new legal ways for retail investors to participate in the market.

[3]The management fees you pay to alternative investment managers probably cannot be used as an offset against your taxable income. As explained on page 5 of Chapter 1, in a low-return environment this could result in a taxable investor paying tax rates well above 50% on the profits generated by a hedge fund or private investment fund.

For taxable investors, that is a much higher standard than for a tax-exempt investor. Setting the right standard will substantially reduce the number of qualifying strategies, structures, and funds. It will also push you to narrow your focus and make you a more discerning buyer.

HEDGE FUNDS ARE RARELY GOOD FOR TAXABLE INVESTORS

The name "hedge fund" suggests that investors can get good returns from publicly traded securities while "hedging" the downside risk, or so the marketing pitch goes. Some hedge funds also claim to be good diversifiers to an equity portfolio. The reality is somewhat different. First of all, not all hedge funds hedge; for the rest, their hedges are imperfect. Sometimes both the aggressive bets and the bets designed as a "hedge" go wrong at the same time. The result can get ugly.

Academics who've studied the claims of hedge fund managers have had their doubts for a long time, and that's before considering tax impact.[4] But it's not that simple. Hedging, by definition, should reduce both downside and upside potential. Hedge funds

---

[4]Clifford S. Asness, Robert J Krail, and John M Liew, "Do Hedge Funds Hedge?" *Journal of Portfolio Management* (Fall 2001). From the article's conclusion: "Intentionally or unintentionally, though, hedge funds appear to price their securities at a lag. These marking problems can downwardly bias simple risk estimates based on monthly returns. *When we account for this effect, we find that the return and diversification benefits vanish for the broad hedge fund universe and many sub-categories* [emphasis added]."

Burton G. Malkiel and Atanu Saha, "Hedge Funds: Risk and Return," *Financial Analysts Journal* 61 (no. 6, 2005). The SSRN abstract states, "From a database that is relatively free of bias, this article provides measures of the returns of hedge funds and of the distinctly non-normal characteristics of the data. The results include risk-adjusted measures of performance and tests of the degree to which hedge funds live up to their claim of market neutrality. The substantial attrition of hedge funds is examined, the determinants of hedge fund demise are analyzed, and results of tests of return persistence are presented. *The conclusion is that hedge funds are riskier and provide lower returns than is commonly supposed* [emphasis added]."

David M. Smith, "Evaluating Hedge Fund Performance," *Hedge Funds: Structure, Strategies and Performance*, Oxford University Press (Forthcoming), June 15, 2016. The abstract states, "Hedge fund return information in published databases is

also have restricted liquidity. So, if you want to use them to diversify it may not be possible to rebalance on a timely basis. For the opportunity to participate, investors pay a hefty management fee plus a share of the profits, no matter how meagre. Most hedge funds have high tracking error, but they also have high portfolio turnover, and they often own securities that are subject to higher tax rates. In other words, with rare exception, hedge funds are not tax efficient. In total, these friction costs usually eat up more than 50% of profits,[5] no matter how good or bad the returns are. It's awfully hard to generate better-than-average net returns in funds that invest predominantly, and trade frequently, in publicly traded securities, after a fee and tax burden of that scale.

PRIVATE EQUITY AND VENTURE MAY BE BETTER

The economics for long-term taxable investors in private equity and venture capital fund investing are somewhat better. Private investment funds are long-term in focus, with typical fund lives of 10 years or more and profits taxed entirely as long-term capital gains. They also have high "tracking error," with the goal of meaningful outperformance. Private investment fund managers' incentives – their "carried interest" structures – do a better job of aligning interests between managers (general partners) and investors (limited partners) because they often offer a "preferred return" to limited partners, and carried interest is paid based upon profits made over the full life of the fund. In contrast, hedge funds rarely have a preferred return and their carried interest

usually self-reported, which is a conflict of interest that produces several reporting biases and inflated published average returns. After adjusting for these biases hedge fund average returns trail equity market returns and in fact almost exactly equal US Treasury bill average returns between January 1994 and March 2016. Yet, after risk adjustment, the hedge fund performance picture brightens. In the aggregate, hedge funds have higher Sharpe ratios and multifactor alphas, and lower maximum drawdown levels than equity market benchmarks."
[5] Stuart Lucas and Alejandro Sanz, "The 50% Rule: Keep More Profit in Your Wallet," *Journal of Wealth Management* 20 (no. 2, Fall 2017). If anything, the subsequently passed Tax Cuts and Jobs Act of 2017 made hedge funds less tax efficient than the figures in this article.

distributions are typically paid annually. In a good year a hedge fund manager gets a big reward; he or she doesn't have to give it back if the following year is a dud.

Private equity incentive structures have their weaknesses too. Pretax, IRR-based incentives can encourage managers to flip businesses for a quick profit, generating a tax bill for us rather than letting strong businesses compound their growth over the longer term. Even at modestly lower IRRs, that longer-term growth is typically better for taxable investors. These days, private companies are being sold from PE firm to PE firm to PE firm – sometimes with interim steps as public companies – growing throughout but enabling the firms to lock in profits and forcing taxable investors to pay tax on capital gains over and over. As one example among many, the retailer Petco was publicly traded 20 years ago. In 2000, it was taken private by TPG and Leonard Green & Partners. Then a few years later it was taken public again, then taken private again by the same consortium, and then, in 2015, sold to another private consortium of CVC Partners and the Canada Pension Plan Investment Board. All the while, the company grew and grew its business. If only TPG and Leonard Green had just held the business for 20 years. The profits would have been massive, the taxes deferred for two decades, the fees paid to investment bankers would have been a fraction of what they were. But the PE firms' partners would have had to wait for their carried interest payouts and tax-exempt institutional investors would only have seen "marked to market" estimates, not realized returns in their performance metrics.

SCALE, STRUCTURE, AND TAX ARE IMPORTANT CONSIDERATIONS

In order to invest directly into an alternative investment fund, you need to meet certain statutory size requirements, such as a minimum of $5 million of financial assets. Many of the most sought-after alternative investment funds designate even higher minimums to discourage smaller investors, even if they statutorily qualify. In recent years, fund distributors have "retailized" alternative investments, enabling much smaller check sizes for some funds. But with retailization comes higher fees. Remember, too, that for most taxable investors, these fees are not tax deductible. You pay tax on pre-fee returns, but your profit only comes to you after fees (and taxes).

Twenty years ago, the average private equity fund outperformed public markets by enough to justify the additional risk and illiquidity. The fishing was good. But that benefit is dissipating with the huge growth in private equity funds and resultant competition.[6] The odds of sufficient outperformance to compensate you for the risks and intrinsic lack of liquidity may still be better than in public markets, but you have to be more selective. How will you compete for access to a shrinking pool of elite funds? Do you have differentiated insights in selecting managers or market subsectors that may be underexploited? Do your advisors? Guessing wrong in the alternatives funds space is more expensive because these funds have a higher "dispersion of returns" than traditional equity and fixed income portfolios. In other words, when things go well, they can do quite well, but the reverse is also true. Plus, your mistakes are much harder to exit than in traditional liquid markets. There is no requirement to play in alternatives, and if you don't have good answers to these questions, you're probably better off remaining on the sidelines.

The tax code provides incentives to taxable investors in certain real estate and venture capital investments. You may hear about §1031 exchanges in real estate, or §1202 qualifying small businesses, or depletion allowances in oil and gas well developments. The most recent 2017 tax bill created Qualified Opportunity Zones. Long-term investments compounding at high rates of return generate big profits and big deferred tax liabilities. Both are good. These tax incentives defer, reduce, or eliminate taxes on profits, but they should come with two warning labels. First, in order to achieve these tax benefits, you need profitable underlying investments. Second, those investments need to be structured properly. Otherwise, the incentives are of no value.

[6]Bain & Co. and McKinsey & Co. both produce annual reports on the private equity industry full of excellent information about the market. These reports may be downloaded free of charge from the companies' websites.

Structuring is a particular issue with certain institutional real estate funds, especially ones with higher return objectives. The way the tax code is written suggests that real estate should be tax efficient. By statute, the tax on real estate rental income can be shielded by accounting depreciation on the property's value. However, when a property is sold, depreciation recapture causes the unpaid tax to become due. If a real estate fund only holds its properties for a few years, the benefit of the depreciation shield is minimal. In addition, few real estate funds employ §1031 exchanges.

Structuring investments to optimize tax can be easier if you are making direct investments one at a time, rather than through a fund. Going this route can be lucrative, but only if you have the networks, scale, experience, and skills to make good investments and nurture them along the path to success. Again, without a good underlying investment, tax incentives are of little value. This is a path that some taxable investors will take with success; many will find the going much tougher. It is easy to make an investment, but lessons learned the hard way can be expensive and the pain can stay with you a long time. I find myself voicing caution much more than encouragement to clients, participants in my University of Chicago Private Wealth Management program and other family offices with whom I speak. Building the necessary infrastructure is expensive, talent retention is challenging, and it's best to "walk before you run."

In summary, many alternative investment funds aren't optimal for taxable investors: hedge funds and real estate funds not optimally structured for taxable investors are examples. In addition, there's greater dispersion of return in alternatives. The funds with the best long-term track records are often closed to new investors or impose very high minimums that put them beyond the reach of most individual investors. Today's furious marketing tempo, fueled by a highly professional and well-compensated intermediary infrastructure, doesn't reflect the diminishing outperformance of these investments versus the wholly liquid public markets.[7] A discerning taxable investor should quickly

[7]My colleague at the University of Chicago's Booth School of Business, Professor Steven N. Kaplan, is possibly the foremost researcher in the world on private

eliminate huge swaths of the alternative investment industry, freeing up time and resources to focus on those sectors, structures, networks, and opportunities where she stands a fighting chance of success.

ARE YOU PREPARED TO INVEST?

Today, most financial advisors offer their clients alternative investments. Keep in mind that offering investments and being a good investor are not the same thing. The former is easy; the latter is much more difficult. Nor is having investment experience the same as being a good investor. The latter is an experienced principal committing capital to risk assets with considerable skill and judgment, having his or her results measured, and riding through the emotional, intellectual, and analytical challenges of alternating periods of good performance and weak performance.

All the investment managers you will consider are experienced investors. But are you? Is your financial advisor? Choosing managers and building a portfolio of managers focused on an array of asset classes is investing: if you are going to invest in high-tracking-error investments, including alternative investments, there should be at least one person on your advisory team who is an experienced, accomplished investor, preferably with a demonstrable track record. Ideally, your team has the confidence to invest their own capital alongside yours – acting as principals serving principals. This is a higher standard than simply engaging someone with years of investment experience to advise you. The latter is necessary but not always sufficient when you are making long-term, irreversible, impactful investment decisions. To have reasonable odds of success, the kind of investment talent you need will not come cheap. The risk of underinvesting in talent is finding that you own a group of assets that perform poorly and that you're stuck with for a decade or more. That's why being fully prepared and fully resourced to enter this fray is so critical.

equity performance. Professor Kaplan's publicly available research on private equity and other topics can be found at https://faculty.chicagobooth.edu/steven.kaplan/research/. Previously cited work by Bain & Co and McKinsey are also good resources.

KEY CHAPTER TAKEAWAYS

- Alternative investments are no longer alternative. They represent large, mature, and increasingly competitive investment segments.
- High fees and poor tax efficiency make almost all hedge funds a poor value proposition for taxable investors, even though they may be a reasonable choice for nontaxable ones.
- The tax and fee profiles of private equity and venture funds are more attractive, but only if investors can tolerate the illiquidity of these investments and have the necessary evaluation skills in what have become highly competitive marketplaces.
- Seek out advisors whose financial interests are aligned with your own and who are experienced investors.
- Investment strategy and fund structure are both important considerations when evaluating alternatives.

CHAPTER TEN

Plan Your Estate: It Adds More Value Than Investing

One of the most important, and at times most challenging decisions that financially successful people need to make is how to share the fruits of their success with others through their estate plans. Estate planning is an essential factor in effective wealth management. If large estates don't legally work to reduce estate tax liability the result is costly, to the tune of up to 40% or more of the value of the estate. Looked at another way, legally minimizing estate tax can be worth more than 2.5 percentage points of investment return each year for 20 years.

Because estate tax laws are rules-based, not market-based, the odds of success are higher and more predictable than generating long-term investment returns of that magnitude. Done right, estate planning is the essence of asymmetry, magnitude, and probability of success. Of course, doing one successfully does not diminish the odds of doing the other.

FIGURE 10.1   CREATE VALUE AT THE INTERSECTIONS.

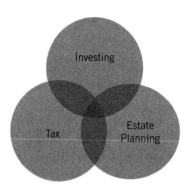

Insufficient planning, on the other hand, can lead to outsized tax bills, potential loss of control of businesses, family strife, inadequate guidance around philanthropic intentions, and other major issues. Negative consequences – almost always unintended – undermine finances, erode business competitiveness, tear at the fabric of families, and hurt community institutions.

In previous chapters, you've read about tax-efficient investing with a specific focus on income and capital gains tax management. Tax-efficient investing makes sense on a stand-alone basis, but its effects are even more powerful when paired with thoughtful estate planning (Figure 10.1).

There are real opportunities for value creation at the intersection of investment, tax, and estate planning, especially when considering asset-based taxes – like estate and gift taxes – as well as income-based taxes. When designing such intersections, the magnitude, asymmetry, correlation, and cash flow of investments need to be matched with the legal characteristics of the estate plans as well as the long-term financial and cultural goals of the family to achieve optimal effect. You also need to account for the fact that the future is uncertain.

There are three ways to optimize estate tax. First, you can reduce the size of a taxable estate by making taxable gifts and non-taxable gifts. Each year you can give up to $15,000, adjusted for inflation, to each of as many people as you like. A couple may give twice this amount. If you have the resources and the inclination you can distribute millions of dollars each year in this way. There is no legal limit to your largesse. You can also pay directly for anyone's educational or medical expenses. You can make gifts to philanthropy. None of these gifts, properly executed, is taxable. Of course, you may give gifts of additional amounts, but they may be subject to gift tax.

Second, you can reduce the value of your estate by a process of discounting, and then transferring those discounted interests. Imposing liquidity constraints on an asset, or reducing or eliminating control rights of an asset, reduces the value of that asset to prospective owners who are encumbered by those restrictions. Imagine that you put some of your assets in a "family limited partnership." In the partnership agreement, you might have good reason to impose severe liquidity and control constraints on the limited partnership interests, reserving full voting control of the underlying assets for the general partner. You can see why an interest in an asset owned indirectly through a limited partner interest that has severely curtailed rights would be worth less than owning the asset unencumbered. The asset contributed to the partnership might be worth $X, but because of the established constraints, a limited partnership interest in the asset could have a value of only a fraction of its proportionate share of the asset. That limited partner interest can then be given to others at a properly reduced value.

Third, you can freeze the estate's value and transfer future appreciation to others. There are various ways to achieve this but one of the more common methods is creating a Grantor Retained Annuity Trust (GRAT). GRATs can be used to transfer to future generations, without any estate tax, the subsequent appreciation in an asset but not the risk. If the asset hasn't appreciated during the life of the GRAT, when the GRAT expires the entire asset simply reverts back to the grantor. In some cases, it may make sense to fund a GRAT with a single restricted stock position, with limited voting rights, in expectation that within the GRAT's life the stock will appreciate. Alternatively, it may make sense to create a series of GRATs with different volatile assets and different time frames. If you have sufficient scale, the additional cost of employing multiple GRATs is likely outweighed by the additional asset and time diversification built into this estate planning strategy. Pairing your GRAT strategy with lifetime trust structures may add more governance control and predictability to the process. Integrating the investment design, tax design, and planning design can create a little magic.

Another tool that could be a hybrid of these methods is an Intentionally Defective Grantor Trust (IDGT), funded with limited partnership interests in a rapidly appreciating but concentrated asset for the benefit of future generations. Once it's time to sell and realize the capital gain, the grantor may have the option (but not the obligation) to pay the trust's tax without gift tax implications, enabling the trust to diversify its assets and reduce risk while shrinking the grantor's estate and eliminating a tax bill for the next generation.

A Charitable Remainder Unit Trust (CRUT) is another interesting tool, especially if you have large unrealized gains. One particular version of this, a "NIMCRUT,"[1] is an irrevocable trust funded with cash or (highly appreciated) assets that makes regular distributions to you or someone you designate, typically for life, and provides you with a charitable tax deduction. The remaining value in the NIMCRUT at death is directed to a charitable institution of your choosing. With a properly structured NIMCRUT, you pay no capital gains tax on the appreciated assets you donated, and you get financial security from the regular distributions from the NIMCRUT no matter how long you live. Numerous universities work with their alumni to establish CRUTs of various kinds that give the donor peace of mind financially and the joy of supporting an institution that is important to them.

As you can see, trusts come in many flavors but most of them are designed 1) to separate ownership from control of an asset, and 2) legally to minimize or eliminate estate tax, in some cases for generations. Often the two objectives are designed into the same trust structure.

It is easy to get wrapped up in the mechanics of estate plans but these tools are most useful when their design is consistent with your personal values, with careful consideration for how your

---

[1] Net Income with Makeup Charitable Remainder Unit Trust.

actions today will impact beneficiaries decades into the future, and with an element of humility about your ability to predict that future. Estate planning tools and techniques have lasting financial *and* emotional impact. You will need good legal advice, coordinated with good tax and investment advice. You will also benefit from commonsense advice that only comes from keen observation and pattern recognition of experience.

Protection against potentially unscrupulous creditors is another concern to many. Certain states have powerful creditor protections to shield trusts or personal residences from being targeted successfully. Just be sure to have your strategy and structures in place well in advance of an actual threat. Waiting until someone sues you to establish such protection is probably going to be too late.

A common, unromantic, but potentially useful form of protection is a prenuptial agreement. The "prenup" negotiation process must include full disclosure of assets and each party to the "prenup" must have independent legal representation. Prenups are complicated affairs, legally and emotionally. I encourage you to get good advice from more than one trusted person, including your lawyer. In addition, if you think your children might benefit from prenups, I encourage you have conversations with them before a prospective spouse is on the horizon. Then the concept can germinate before it becomes personal.

Estate and tax planning almost invariably create rigidities and can increase illiquidity. In an uncertain world, poor design can substantially increase risk. In the quest to earn more, I've seen people reach too far for profit without contemplating low-probability, unintended outcomes. In one case, an entrepreneur sold some highly appreciated, but illiquid, stock in one company and reinvested all the proceeds in another highly promising venture-backed business. He didn't set aside money to pay the taxes because he expected his original company shortly to go public at an even higher price, enabling him to sell more stock to pay the tax. But before the company could IPO, the dotcom bubble burst, and the liquidity event never materialized. However, the taxes on the sale were still due and he had no cash to pay them. The transactions' designers confused "white money" (a stock certificate: sometimes illiquid and always volatile) with "green money" (cash) and created a terrible mess.

I've also seen unintended, low-probability consequences work the opposite way. A GRAT funded with a single stock that then soared in value made the grantors' children and grandchildren much wealthier, much faster, and with little or no effort of their own, than the grantor ever intended.

Another risk is that people and institutions change. The best way to counter estate plan rigidities in the face of change is to embed flexible governance provisions into trust documents and to choose trustees who can knowledgeably assert their authority. Trustees are responsible for following the law as it evolves, while applying a duty of care to current and future beneficiaries as they mature and face life's vicissitudes. Because trustees inevitably have evolving strengths and weaknesses of their own, every estate plan should include a process by which board directors, trustees, and others involved in governance, whether individuals or companies, are periodically evaluated by or on behalf of grantors and beneficiaries. A "Trust Protector" should be charged with, and have the capacity to, replace people and institutions in positions of governance. Having a Trust Protector provision will not only help to fix problems, but it will make it less likely that serious problems arise in the first place: the incentives align for everyone to perform in the grantors' and beneficiaries' best interest.

A trust charges trustees to interpret and fulfill the directions expressed in a grantor's instructions, some of which are legally binding. Other instructions may be guidelines subject to interpretation. Trustees must also balance the interests between current and future beneficiaries. All these responsibilities must be fulfilled in a legal environment that specifies rigorous duties of trustees and makes them liable if they don't perform. This is a hard job best executed by trusted, experienced professionals.

As assets transfer from generation to generation, trusts tend to proliferate. In order to optimize estate plans, asset ownership divides among the growing number of beneficiaries, often with multiple trusts for each beneficiary. Simultaneously, there may be good business reasons to concentrate governance control of key family assets in just a few hands. Trusts are well suited for addressing this dichotomy: with a trust, the economic interest in a family business can be divided countless times while one or a handful of trustees can have voting control over the entire family stake. The same could apply to a family vacation property or art collection. Especially when assets are hard or impossible to divide, a mechanism of governance based on broad voting or, worse yet, complete individual autonomy, could be a disaster. Better to have governance that recognizes leadership, encourages compromise for common good, expects professionalism, and requires shared accountability with appropriate transparency. Good trust structures can make the difference between good decision making and paralysis, between maintaining family control of a valuable asset and losing it.

Make sure you and your estate planning attorney think through, and appropriately memorialize, trust governance structure. Good planning can stave off expensive litigation down the road. Well-crafted documents interpreted by competent trustees can add tremendous value and/or prevent unintended erosion of value. Establishing good trust structures and good governance is important, but the challenge doesn't end there.

For their effectiveness to be optimized, trusts require infrastructure and excellent recordkeeping, especially as the strategies and record keeping get more complex and time horizons lengthen. Each individual trust must be managed separately. But it's also important to contextualize each within a coherent understanding of the whole family enterprise. Finally, communication of the trusts' characteristics and purposes to the beneficiaries is essential. Adult beneficiaries should be regularly informed about trusts for their benefit, as well as other key elements of the family enterprise and its long-term financial performance. Good communication underpins healthy family culture.

These supports are best provided through the professional application of disciplined processes executed in a secure environment at scale. They can be provided at reasonable cost by qualified trust banks. Some financial advisory firms have dedicated trust companies to provide these services as well. Only the largest and most complex families have sufficient scale to establish professional single-family offices – and sometimes private trust companies – to provide these services.

There are other potential benefits at the intersection of investing, tax, and estate planning. Under current tax law, deferred tax liabilities retained in one's estate at the time of death are more valuable than ever. Today, you can bequeath up to $11.4 million of your assets without paying federal estate tax; a married couple gets $22.8 million.[2] Those $11.4 million in assets could have a cost basis approaching zero and therefore a deferred capital gains tax liability of nearly $3 million, or modestly more depending on state-level taxes. If assets are bequeathed at death, that tax liability disappears, and the estate beneficiaries receive those $11.4 million on a "stepped-up basis." Once the beneficiaries own the assets, only incremental appreciation above the $11.4 million will ever be subject to capital gains tax. Assets with values above $11.4 million are subject to federal, and in some cases state, estate tax. The tax is applied to asset value, not the amount of capital gain, and the rate is higher. However, net assets above the $11.4 million also receive stepped-up basis.

Alternatively, you may give away some, or all, of the $11.4 million while you are alive without having to pay gift tax.[3] Giving away an asset now that you expect to appreciate considerably can be very generous and save enormous estate tax years or decades into the future. This "Lifetime Exemption" is often used to place appreciating assets into trusts for the benefit of others (make sure you keep good records of the cost basis of your gifts; otherwise the recipients will end up paying capital gains on the whole amount of the gift when it comes time to sell). There are important downsides to consider in determining whether to use your Lifetime Exemption. If you make gifts using your Lifetime Exemption, beneficiaries don't benefit from the stepped-up basis and the gifts that you make now reduce dollar for dollar the amounts you can bequeath at death with a stepped-up basis.

---

[2] This estate tax exemption and the Lifetime Exemption amounts are temporary and currently sunset in 2026. In the meantime, their size adjusts annually for inflation.

[3] Above a $15,000 (in 2019) "annual exclusion" per gift recipient, gift tax rates are generally comparable to estate tax rates, so they are high. Gifts above $15,000 to any individual can be applied to the donor's Lifetime Exemption, but that amount is calculated per donor, not per gift recipient.

Regardless of the size of your estate, good estate planning starts with having a valid will that ensures that you can dispose of all your assets as you choose. At your death, good planning can protect your privacy by keeping your assets out of probate court, away from public scrutiny, and potentially protected from potential litigants.

Talk with your advisors about all these and other estate planning tools: understand the details, develop plans, and then make sure they don't just sit on a shelf. Recognize there are tradeoffs between retaining control and flexibility on the one hand and ceding control, achieving tax savings, but infusing long-term rigidities on the other. When you've determined your plans, implement them through a professionally managed infrastructure, monitor your progress, and review the underlying documents periodically to make sure they are still operating consistent with your objectives.

KEY CHAPTER TAKEAWAYS

- Regardless of the wealth you have, consider estate planning a key component of your investment strategy. With the right legal, tax, and investment advice, plus excellent recordkeeping, you can add more value with a higher probability of success than through trying to beat the market.
- Managing the intersections of investment, tax, and estate planning can be powerfully positive. You want to be able to optimize the compound effect of these three disciplines working in harmony, not have one counteract the benefits of another.
- Estate planning, tax planning, and certain investment strategies can each create illiquidity and rigidity. When managing the intersections, make sure to align the strategy with levels of leverage and liquidity to avoid unintended consequences.
- Be prepared for the fragmentation that comes from estate planning. How will you manage that complexity now and in the future?

CHAPTER ELEVEN

Shift from Success to Significance

Wealth without values is just money. As you grow businesses, as your career matures, as you accumulate significant financial assets, and as you age, how are you going to organize your affairs? Once you have built financial security, what will you do with your business, your time, and your money to maximize their intrinsic value to your family and to society?

In his book *Just Enough*,[1] Howard Stevenson – my good friend, consummate Harvard Business School professor, record-breaking fund raiser, superb investor, and prolific author – explores the path from success to significance. He asks, "How can I make a positive impact on people, institutions, and issues I care most about?" It's a great question.

Live your values. Values are what bring meaning to your accumulated assets, and values will define how you deploy those assets, in life and in death. Values are among the most important

---

[1] Howard Stevenson and Laura Nash, *Just Enough: Tools for Creating Success in Your Work and Life* (John Wiley & Sons, 2005).

attributes we can share with our children, who will observe not what we say about our values, but what we do to express them.

This chapter starts with some important but mechanistic topics. Stick with me; as the chapter moves along, the topics get juicier.

For me, providing some protection to my family in an uncertain world is something to aspire to. One tool for building security is insurance. Sufficiently insuring our cars, our homes, and our health is a good idea and is sometimes a legal requirement. Insuring our lives can be equally important. In a household with one or more major breadwinners, if that person can no longer work due to illness or disability, or dies, there is not only the risk of substantial medical costs but also the loss of future income. I've seen such a loss throw a family from a trajectory of substantial wealth creation into complete financial turmoil. Disability insurance is expensive. It may be a good solution in some situations; in others the cost may not warrant the benefit. On the other hand, term life insurance doesn't provide complete protection, but is competitively priced and relatively inexpensive for healthy people who are in their thirties, forties, and fifties. Of course, as you age, the cost rises. Especially in situations when a household is dependent on one breadwinner, having a substantial term life insurance policy on that person's life can be good planning. The probabilities of needing it are small but the benefits (think magnitude) of having it, if needed, is huge. The payoff is classically asymmetrical.

Whole life or universal life insurance policies are sold as tools for avoiding income and estate tax, often by life insurance specialists who are incentivized to sell life insurance, not necessarily to find the best integrated investment, tax, and estate planning solution for you. Be very careful and sweat the details before making a decision to buy. The structures of whole life or universal life products are highly complicated, restrictive, and laden with incentive sales fees, not to mention ongoing investment management and insurance costs. Many life insurance policies lapse before being paid out. Lapsed policies are highly profitable to the insurers.

Policies are sold using "illustrations" of future performance: the reader sees steadily growing value in the policy and declining payments over the insured's projected lifespan. If the life insurance industry were regulated by the Federal Securities and Exchange Commission (the SEC) instead of state-by-state insurance regulators, these illustrations would not be allowed: the illustrations are definitely not guarantees. They are subject to revision over the policy's life at the behest of the insurance company, driven by a combination of the insurer's managerial skill, shifts in actuarial tables, policy lapse rates, market circumstances, and other factors, manageable and unforeseen. Insurers have rigid and expensive rules if you want to surrender or switch your policy, especially in the retail market. Every illustration I've seen assumes that estate and income taxes don't change; I've never seen a sensitivity analysis that explores changing rates. Illustrations don't address counterparty risk either. If you own a life insurance policy, you are a general creditor of the insurance company. If it goes bust, your policy could be toast. Do you have the option to change insurers at any time? In other words, is your policy "portable"?

Private placement life insurance (PPLI) provides relief to some costs and restrictions, but you must commit many millions of dollars to qualify. PPLI, as it's sometimes referred to, may be useful for specific planning purposes either to reduce taxes associated with some investment strategies or to ensure sufficient liquidity to pay estate taxes for highly illiquid estates, like ones that include a private business that a family wishes to control for generations.

If you wish to pursue whole life or universal life policies as estate planning and investment tools, make sure you have experienced, ethical advisors in your corner to help with investigating and deciding upon alternatives. Make sure you ask, "Is there another more flexible and less expensive alternative?"

On a more enthusiastic note, supporting philanthropic organizations is another way to make a positive impact on people, institutions, and issues you care about. You can provide financial support to causes you believe in, or write checks in support of your friends' causes, and receive almost instantaneous psychic and social benefit. Many philanthropic organizations – especially smaller, local ones – are underresourced and they truly appreciate every dollar you send their way.

The mechanics of giving them money are a bit mundane but important nonetheless. Donating highly appreciated securities instead of cash invokes the government to share more fully in giving the gift, while lowering your taxes.[2] It leverages the size and value of your gift. So does responding to, or establishing, well-thought-out matching gift programs.

There are many ways to give. You can make outright gifts to qualified 501(c)(3) charitable organizations. For greater flexibility and control, you can establish a private foundation. However, you have to administer your foundation and there are more restrictions on the tax deductibility of gifts you make to the foundation relative to your income. You are also required to distribute at least 5% of the foundation's assets each year. Alternatively, you may create and make donations to a personal "fund" within a "donor-advised fund" platform and decide later whether and how much of your "fund" you will recommend giving away each year, and to which qualified organizations. Many large financial institutions, including Fidelity, Vanguard, and Schwab, offer donor-advised funds. They are easy to administer and the costs are low.

It is important to distinguish between philanthropy, which is largely about donating money, and public service, which is largely about donating time. Many of us find it gratifying to work directly on causes that are important to us, that improve the lives of others, and that strengthen our communities. Public institutions need strong, effective governance as well as volunteers working with passion in the proverbial trenches. Investing our financial resources in conjunction with our time can be the most impactful strategy of all, both to the institutions we serve and to others who might look

[2]Using highly appreciated securities instead of cash to make philanthropic grants increases the government's stake in your gifting because capital gains tax that would otherwise go to the government goes to the grantee. This book's investment strategy can be integrated with your philanthropic strategy. For example, in time, your tax-managed indexed portfolio will generate highly appreciated stocks. You can select a stock from the portfolio with a cost basis of $20 and a market value of $100. If you were to sell the stock, you would pay roughly $20 of capital gains tax on $80 of profit. You're left with $80 to give away on which you can get a tax deduction. Instead, if you give away the $100 worth of stock, you get a tax deduction on the full $100, the charity gets the full $100, and you pay no capital gains tax. The US government allows this to encourage its citizens to be philanthropic.

to us for civic leadership. Our leadership can inspire others in our networks to be more generous with their time and treasure. Our children will watch our commitment to others; there may even be opportunities to work together in the service of others. Sharing a commitment to public service through time and dollars can build or strengthen affinities within families that can last for decades, sometimes generations.

You can have a positive impact making gifts closer to home, too. Use estate planning tools to augment the expression of your values. 529 plans are great ways to support the education of your children and grandchildren. You can also directly pay unlimited educational and medical expenses for others – immediate family or not – without triggering gift tax. Encourage your working children to put as much money as they can into tax-deferred or tax-exempt (Roth) retirement plans. Through deferred tax compounding, $1,000 contributed today could be worth $50,000 in retirement 50 years from now. If you have the financial capacity, as an added incentive to save, consider using your own $15,000 "annual exclusion gift allowances" to "reimburse" some of the cash that your children are socking away, on a tax-preference basis, for the future. Encouraging savings into Roth IRAs, especially when children's tax rates are low, rewards hard work, lets them observe and learn from a powerful compounding tool early in adulthood, and reinforces good savings habits early.

How we live our lives and how we deploy the capital we've built give our success meaning. If we live our values, we can strengthen family ties, restore or reinforce vibrant communities, and make the world a better place.

KEY CHAPTER TAKEAWAYS

- Wealth without values is just money. If you live your values, they can bring meaning to your accumulated assets and make your life richer.
- Protect and encourage family with a range of tools, including term life insurance; early, aggressive use of retirement plans; 529 education plans; and annual exclusion gifts.

- Giving your time through public service and your treasure through philanthropy are important expressions of your values, and powerful tools for making the world a better place. Leading by example also helps children and grandchildren to learn, collaborate, and crystallize family priorities for impact, setting a stage for the perpetuation of your values for generations.

CHAPTER TWELVE

Reinforce Positive Family Culture through Financial Design

F amilies with multigenerational perspectives to managing wealth can use this book as a guide to grow their assets across generations, but they need to build the right culture alongside. As we've seen, the investment choices are stark. They can invest to minimize short-term volatility (what is generally considered "conservative investing"). With this strategy, an investor may gain comfort and a sense of security in the short run, but the math dictates that they will preside over a declining corpus in the long term.[1] Or they can invest most of their assets in equities, public or private, and have a decent chance to succeed if they remain resolute through the market's ups and downs and through the vicissitudes of life.

With either approach, most of the financial risk in families with great wealth is borne by younger or even unborn

---

[1] Stuart Lucas, *Wealth: Grow It and Protect It,* 2nd ed. (FT Press, 2013), Chapter 4.

generations. Of course, in most multigenerationally wealthy families, we have the good fortune to be talking about relative, not existential, risk. An appropriate understanding of this risk by those younger generations can instill in them a healthy and measured sense of insecurity that encourages risk taking, financial independence, resourcefulness, and the self confidence that blossoms from earned success, in whatever field that success is realized. Who doesn't want that for their children? The greater their resilience in the face of uncertainty and the more productive they are, the less they need your money. Ironically, their increased independence from inherited wealth helps to create the conditions in which that wealth is most likely to grow.

To me, one of the greatest privileges of wealth is the opportunity for second chances. Second chances are a privilege that can come to anyone through a caring teacher, an empathic police officer or courtroom judge, an insightful physical therapist or social worker, or an employer with solid HR policies. But there is no question that having resources hugely raises the odds of getting those second chances when we make stupid mistakes, get unlucky, or simply want a second bite of the proverbial apple.

Wealthy families can prioritize "defensive" support for their children over other kinds of financial support, especially in the first three to four decades of their offspring's lives. That support creates more opportunity for second chances in real time. Helping to "play defense" can mean covering a child's – or grandchild's – education costs, whether paying for test prep and a second chance to take the SATs, or unburdening children from student loans. It can mean covering healthcare costs if the three sessions with the therapist covered by insurance are insufficient. It may mean offering incentives that encourage saving. Contributing to IRAs, 401(k)s, or 403(b)s and other pension plans today can help to finance far distant retirement.

Younger members of wealthy families, imbued with the knowledge that they will need to seek success, however measured, in their own careers can reinforce a family's mission to sustain the wealth across generations. Simply waiting to inherit rarely equates with a sense of accomplishment or of personal fulfillment. The financial behavioral goal is that children, observing their parents' leadership, continue to exhibit healthy wealth management behaviors: managing their own cash flow carefully, growing individual or family investment portfolios under their supervision, passing the corpus to their children on a stepped-up basis, and establishing trusts and philanthropic vehicles. Coordinated and managed diligently, the combined benefits can be worth amounts greater than can be achieved from the act of investing per se. More important than the financial efficiency and effectiveness are disciplined management, learning from mistakes, second chances, and a balance of shared family purpose and individual freedom. Together, these establish an environment and a set of values where people can flourish, feel competent and useful, be challenged, and contribute economically and societally.

Financial design must be flexible enough to address changes in family structure and culture. Not all siblings or cousins work well together. Parents and children don't always see eye to eye on issues big or small. Design elements of investment ownership, estate planning, growth objectives, spending patterns, or even risk tolerance can help to reinforce family unity in powerfully positive ways. But they also should be flexible enough to change with evolving realities of family dynamics. Sometimes shared assets get divided and divided, to the point where managing them as one becomes impractical. Different career paths, different numbers of children, different spousal interests, death, disability, divorce, or different personalities can drive people apart. Then there are the risks of human fallibility or transgressions that can cause all sorts of problems. When the distances become great enough, it may be time to divide assets and encourage one, some, or all adult family members to go their separate ways.

Family culture can reach a critical juncture when a family sells a long-held family business. For better or worse, business ownership imposes financial discipline: careful consideration of reinvestment versus distribution of cash and profits, the visible impact of hard work and the value of talent, a sense that the family serves the business rather than vice versa, and joint accountability among family members. In the transition from business-owning family to "financial family," these fiscal virtues and cultural inheritances can be tested. We work with our business-owning clients to address such issues in their post-liquidity event planning, structuring, and communication.

Finally, and critically, when planning multigenerationally, it is more valuable than ever to integrate that long-term equity investment strategy with estate planning that encourages deferred gratification, including prudent spending and aggressive saving. Good planning also lays the foundation for smooth transitions of governance from generation to generation as well as designs for shared accountability that encourage a balance of personal independence with compromise for the greater family good. Getting the balance right is important. Substantial wealth, coupled with inexperience in managing it and complete autonomy, is rarely a recipe for success.

When I teach, speak to, and work with wealthy families, I encourage them to get comfortable being uncomfortable. Financial markets are volatile, and so are businesses. Economic and political cycles can add to a sense of unease that accompanies volatility. Personal and family circumstances change. Building a tolerance for volatility and even a capacity to see opportunity in that volatility are healthy. Resilience and opportunism can keep us sharp and motivate us. One of the ways we can get comfortable being uncomfortable is to train ourselves to think and act long-term and to ignore short-term ups and downs.

We work together with our clients to build effective communication about family values as well as family wealth because we know that cultural assets are essential building blocks for successful families with multigenerational wealth. They are every bit as important to flourishing families as their business and financial assets, and in the long run probably more so.

KEY CHAPTER TAKEAWAYS

- Get comfortable being uncomfortable. Think and act long-term. Consider challenging your family to re-create the wealth in each generation.
- Financial success dramatically increases the odds of second chances. Be grateful.

- A level of financial uncertainty is good in wealthy families and a motivator to engage with the world productively. Ambition, self-reliance, and compassion for others are cultural assets that are essential building blocks for successful multigenerational families. They are every bit as important as business and financial assets, and in the long run probably more so.
- Instill in your children the value of earning their own keep. Independent career success reinforces one's sense of self-worth, builds resiliency, and supports the growth of family wealth.
- Flourishing families are as intentional about communication and culture – and the actions that express them – as with investment strategy.
- Thoughtful financial design, planning, and communication reinforce a family's essential cultural elements.

CHAPTER THIRTEEN

Evaluate the Risks to This Approach

This manifesto explains the rationale for a long-term, equity-heavy, business-building, tax-efficient, leakage-controlled, patient approach to wealth management for taxable investors. It is a call to action that I do not take lightly. I am committed to it, my family is committed to it, and so are my other clients. They are people working hard to build businesses, financial security, and cultures in which their families can flourish. Of course, my approach can't guarantee results. But implementing these practices will raise the odds of success significantly higher than for any alternative I've seen in over 35 years of practice.

When assessing risks, it's important to evaluate the path you've chosen; it is also important to compare it with reasonable alternatives. So what are the biggest risks to executing this strategy? I see two: permanent impairment of capital and a confiscatory tax code. I have touched on both of these risks throughout the book, but here they are again in a single place.

There are four most likely causes of permanent impairment of capital. First is the risk of a structural decline in corporate profits that leads to a decline in equity valuations that is never followed by a recovery. For the last 200 years, through world wars, disease epidemics, and great depressions, the world has experienced tremendous productivity growth, rises in standards of living, growth in population, declines in war-driven casualties, and many other factors that have supported global profit growth and the rise in equity markets. Looking forward, there is reason to be hopeful that these trends will persist. But the future is uncertain and there have been exceptions on a country-by-country basis. Most recently, Japan's stock market today is roughly half its peak value in 1989 and corporate profitability is low and stagnant. Argentina was one of the 10 richest countries in the world in 1900; it's been a tale of missed opportunity ever since.[1]

Today, we face the risk that global warming could send sharp shockwaves through our hydrocarbon-based economy, corporate profits, and our current way of life. Since the Gutenberg press (and probably before), technology and productivity enhancements have been a threat to employment and to political stability, but the threat may be getting more acute. Some forecasters believe that technology deployments could put half the population out of work in the next fifty years. If we can't solve the issues associated with proliferating technology, the implications for profits, capital investment, fulfilling employment opportunities, political processes, and an open society are ominous. On the other hand, advancing technology and improved infrastructure have ameliorated past threats like famine, smallpox, and runaway population growth.

Demographic headwinds in countries like Japan, Spain, and China are putting added stress on pensions, social security, healthcare, and other entitlements. Negative interest rates in some countries are getting lots of press. If they were to become pervasive and structural, might that be a cause of some fundamental revaluation of markets and corporate profitability? I am cautiously optimistic we can navigate all these threats, and new ones too. It makes a sound investment approach as important as it's ever been.

---

[1] "A Century of Decline: The Tragedy of Argentina," *Economist*, February 17, 2014.

A second cause of permanent impairment is that the equity risk premium soars and stays high. Investment theory suggests that equity investors need incentives to take risk. In other words, they must believe they will get better returns for taking more risk. If equity investors get cold feet and demand even greater returns for the risk they take, it will cause stock markets to decline. Such a change in attitude is often associated with a decline in corporate profits. That combination is usually what drives bear markets. Eventually, equities become cheap enough that equity investors pile back in, markets begin to rise again, and a stronger economy drives growing dividends. We've experienced soaring risk premia; in the past they have actually laid the seeds of market recovery, not foretold doom, but that is not a guarantee.

A third potential cause of permanent impairment is that you deviate from your investment strategy at precisely the wrong time. Of course, we are all vulnerable to changing personal or family circumstances: families grow, people get sick, mistakes are made, you get unlucky. Sometimes a change of strategy is warranted independent of market volatility. But if you panic in the face of a bear market and sell, you will lose the opportunity to enjoy the bull market that follows. Suffering a decline, then selling near the bottom and missing the market's recovery, is a great destroyer of wealth. Even with awareness of the risk, people fall victim to doing this in every cycle, making a mistake from which they may never recover. That's one reason why it is so important to not overspend, keep leverage modest, and stay the course.

A fourth related cause is the excessive direct, indirect, or naïve use of leverage. Wealth management is a long-term game and leverage can knock you out before you get to the finish line. Leverage comes in many forms and structures. How much debt do you have in your business? Is it structured sufficiently conservatively to withstand a downturn and sufficiently aggressively to keep management sharp? Hedge funds and private equity embed leverage into their strategies. Do you know how your managers are structuring their debt? Can one bad investment within a fund cause the whole fund to collapse? It happens. Astute investors prepare for individual bumps in the road, but they also need to consider the potential cascade effects of leverage. Are you using margin debt with insufficient collateral to weather a market downturn? Margin accounts are marked to market every day; you can get a margin call at any time if you're not careful. If you must meet a margin call with appreciated securities, the call will also trigger tax payments and exacerbate your pain.

Investing naïvely in derivative securities can also cause harm. Some derivatives can be like their own overleveraged margin account. Some are also subject to two other related risks: unanticipated illiquidity and counterparty risk. This was a lesson learned the hard way in the 2008–2009 financial crisis. Likewise, seemingly robust financial firms can go bankrupt; most employees, even senior ones, were shocked when Lehman Brothers filed for bankruptcy. That bankruptcy coursed through the financial system, causing a great deal of financial and personal pain, ruining people along the way. Financial markets are cyclical by their nature and as a long-term investor you need to plan to weather the inevitable storms and see things through to the other side. Investors who stretch for too much yield or that extra bit of return are particularly susceptible to getting clobbered when things turn against them.

The second major risk is confiscatory changes to the tax structure. Concentration of wealth in fewer and fewer hands, fiscal promiscuity, war, and other factors cause governments to raise taxes. Raising tax on income, whether earned or from investments, hurts workers and investors proportionately. That's not the case with capital gains or estate taxes, which only directly impact the owners of appreciated taxable assets. The more successful you are at building your net assets and your deferred taxes today, the greater the price you could pay if capital gains taxes or estate taxes are raised.

Confiscatory taxes have more than personal consequences; they can cause the whole economy to suffer unduly by sapping entrepreneurial spirit, undermining investment, and damaging financial markets. It's not beyond the realm of possibility that capital impairment risks and confiscatory tax risks are interrelated and could mushroom simultaneously. That is definitely a risk.

To take a full measure of risk one must also assess the road not taken. I suspect the biggest criticisms of this book will come from those who think it espouses a strategy that is too risky. For some, this is no doubt true. If you have a relatively short-term time horizon, or a personal disposition that simply cannot withstand the volatility of stock market prices, or you are not concerned about maintaining or growing your assets and purchasing power, my approach is not right for you. But understand that pursuing a more conservative alternative comes at a cost. Before making a final decision about how to invest, study the cost of that conservative alternative.[2] A portfolio that includes a large portion of relatively low return, tax-inefficient assets will decline in real value over time especially if you're spending from it. The higher your spending rate from these assets, the faster they will decline. Inflation and taxes will also eat away at the value of your assets and erode your purchasing power.

Every investment, and every investment strategy, carries the promise of profits and the risk of loss. Wall Street and academia measure risk and results in pretax percentages, and they design client portfolios based on those metrics. For taxable investors those metrics and design elements are fundamentally flawed. Our goals are different, our circumstances are different. We have to think differently if we want to optimize our investment strategies and our results. The best opportunities for retaining and growing taxable wealth incorporate and integrate investment strategy, tax management, cash flow, and estate planning. If we can reinforce our values, including positive family culture, in our wealth management process so much the better. That's what good taxable investing is all about. Let's practice it and demand it of our advisors.

KEY CHAPTER TAKEAWAYS

* No investment strategy is without risk. It is useful to identify the key risks in advance.
* Assess individual risks and the potential for cascading risk.

[2]You can review the likely outcomes of various combinations of portfolio risk, taxes, inflation, and spending by reading Chapter 4 of *Wealth*, applying the inputs to your own circumstances, and seeing if you are comfortable with the likely outcomes. Some financial advisors also have after-tax models that can help you assess the possibilities based on your personal ambitions and circumstances.

- One big risk of this manifesto's approach is permanent impairment of capital. The sources of risk can be the macro economy, changing your investment strategy at the wrong time, or excessive or naïve risk taking in your own enterprise.

- The other big risk of this approach is a confiscatory tax structure.

- The best opportunities for retaining and growing taxable wealth incorporate and integrate our values, investment strategy, tax management, estate planning, and cash flow controls.

CHAPTER FOURTEEN

Select an Advisor with Strong Investment Skills, an Interdisciplinary Approach, and a Fiduciary Mindset

This manifesto describes an interconnected and interactive tool kit to add value to taxable wealth. At a high level, these techniques apply to every taxable investor. To optimize the tool kit's value, you should seek to adapt and apply those techniques to suit your particular financial circumstances and long-term goals.

Taxable investing is complicated, but it doesn't have to be hard. Great value can be created through integration of long-term, equity-oriented investing, customized tax management, and thoughtful estate planning. Each on its own has the potential to add value. However, as you've read throughout this book, you've seen the potential for real magic to happen at the intersections of these three disciplines. The positive asymmetry of equity returns becomes the dominant feature of your portfolio, the magnitude of returns grows as the effects of tax-deferred compounding kick in, and you can apply cash flow management, tax management, and estate planning techniques that grow and protect your asset base with a high probability of success. Through effective governance and communication, you can reinforce these disciplines with a flourishing family culture – one with intentionally articulated purpose – potentially far into the future.

Sadly, such synchronicity too frequently is the exception in the world of wealth advising. Far too often these disciplines exist in silos, or not at all, without exploiting the truly remarkable power of managing at their intersections. Today, there is still way too much emphasis on beating the market, both by clients and their advisors, in large part because they lack the tools to measure the myriad other ways advisors add tremendous value. There is a better way. I hope both clients and advisors now see the path to break free from this loser's game. Things have already started to change. Last summer, the CFA Institute, the premier global association for investment professionals, overhauled its curriculum on taxable investing to prepare new CFA Charter holders more fully to serve their taxable clients. I hope existing CFA Charter holders, other financial advisors, and the firms that employ them will engage in more rigorous professional development to serve more effectively the special needs of taxable investors and to more comprehensively measure those advisors' value added.

Having a properly focused wealth advisor is beneficial, even if you are comfortable as a do-it-yourself investor and you've determined that a simpler approach to wealth management outlined in Chapters 1 to 7 is right for you. Think of a personal trainer analogy. Even if you are disciplined about getting and staying in shape, there is still a role for your trainer. First of all, a good trainer can help you devise a plan of action, concrete milestones, and a set of long-term goals. He or she can teach you technique and give feedback about whether you're doing things correctly. Some days you need extra motivation as you work toward your goals, especially when you have inevitable setbacks. Your trainer is attuned to how the world changes and how you are changing. He or she stays up on the latest research and shares those parts most relevant to you, and holds you accountable to your own health. Teamwork helps to prevent injury, and if you tweak a muscle in training or twist an ankle on the field of play, your trainer can point you to the right doctor, chiropractor, or therapist. For many clients, a personal trainer's greatest value is to help keep you strong and on track toward your goals.

Think of your financial advisor in the same way. Instead of a workout plan, you need an investment policy statement (IPS). In essence, your IPS is a thoughtful, strategic plan for managing your financial assets. It should articulate your (and your advisor's) commitment to the long-term, low-turnover, tax-efficient, equity-oriented investment strategy articulated in previous chapters. It is really important to codify the long-term nature of your investment strategy, your recognition of short-term market swings, and your willingness to ride through periods of volatility without panicking. At points of stress, both you and your advisor will benefit enormously from being reminded of the commitments you each have made to stay the course through challenging times. Building resolve to persevere is like building muscle, making you stronger in the face of adversity. A good IPS and regular "training" from your advisor adds enormous value. But good and regular are critical; you won't have a useful document or a valuable relationship if your IPS is just a compliance-mandated checklist.

Your IPS is a plan to which all parties can be held account-able. You are establishing a system that gives you comfort that your portfolio is operating according to plan, and early warning signs when it is not. It should describe your asset allocation targets and investment return goals on both an absolute and a relative basis so you can measure your progress in concrete fashion. It can also codify that your advisor's sources of revenue will be transparent to you, unencumbered by conflicts of interest, and reflective of the complexity of your relationship and the size of your assets.

A good client/advisor relationship is about more than just a good IPS. Your advisor, whether an individual or a team, should be a well-organized financial administrator and a solid generalist in wealth management so you can use them as the financial equivalent to a personal trainer. In addition to being trusted and strategic thinkers, they should be good listeners and constructive partners in the management of your financial affairs. If your assets are modest or you're early in your career, try to build up three to six months of salary in cash and set it aside for emergencies as you are also adding to your regular or Roth retirement plan. When you build more annual saving capacity than can reasonably be deployed in retirement plans, ask your advisor to help start your taxable equity portfolio. Until you have millions of dollars set aside for retirement, whether taxable or tax-deferred, your financial affairs are best kept simple. I recommend using, at most, a few broad-based, low-fee, equity index funds or ETFs and maybe a high-quality bond fund or two. Alternatively, many people are experimenting with low-cost robo-advisors that build indexed portfolios on behalf of clients. They have a very interesting value proposition and establishing an account and regularly contributing to it is easy and can be done with modest sums. Now, even large firms are starting to offer services in this space at very low cost.

If your employment circumstances cause you to own interests in a private company or deferred compensation, possibly in the form of options or restricted stock, things get more complicated. Make sure your advisor is experienced or knows where to seek out the specifics you need. More generally, when it comes to implementing the details, they should be able to help you identify when you need specialist skill and help direct you to it.

In any case, your advisor should communicate quarterly to you in writing with clear, concise performance reporting. Advisors' performance reports should be specific to your financial circumstances. At minimum, each report should show your aggregate recent and long-term performance compared to a blended benchmark of broad indexes reflective of your portfolio's risk profile. Some discussion of each manager's performance and the overall tax efficiency of your portfolio should also be incorporated. Many wealth owners relate better to growth in their dollars than growth in percentages, so I recommend that both be presented in a straightforward and thoughtful manner. This is not too much to ask of your advisor; to me it is the acceptable minimum standard. Once a year on an Excel spreadsheet I build a personal balance sheet of all my financial assets and I record how those assets have grown over the years. It's easy, instructive, and good discipline. You can do the same.

If there isn't a lot of activity in your portfolio, you may choose not to speak with your advisor every quarter; you will have a written record that should speak for itself. On the other hand, you and your advisors may communicate between quarterly check-ins to address cash flow or other timely matters, including new investment decisions. Once every year or two, you should set aside time for a strategic discussion about financial and sometimes personal or business matters and a review of your IPS. Once or twice a decade you may change your IPS. It's an important decision, usually based on your changing circumstances, not in response to near-term market volatility. If you have material assets, prepare a will when you marry. It can be simple but have one and talk with your spouse about it. As you have children and build more success in mid-career, start developing an estate plan, consider 529 plans for you children, and annual exclusion gifts and/or trusts. As you build a more complex estate plan, make sure that every five to seven years you review documents and strategy with your advisor and, if appropriate, have them updated.

Many advisors have 50 to 200 clients, or more, depending on average client size. Respect the fact that the advisor has an entire client base to serve. A client who uses my time efficiently and respectfully is a good client. The reverse is true as well.

If you have sufficient financial assets and you've chosen to pursue the active investment strategy articulated in Chapters 8 and 9 to create incremental value, you are entering a highly competitive investment environment populated by smart, hungry people operating in what is at best a zero-sum game. Unless you have a particular expertise, I wouldn't do it with less than $25 million in financial assets. Despite your larger scale, this approach carries higher investment management fees, higher advisor fees, and more tax issues. It's more complicated and more expensive to reach for above-average returns and to build a robust accountability system. If you aren't an investor, you need access to a person or team with that skill, capture sufficient of their brain space, and align interests with them.

If you have enough financial assets – I would say a minimum of $500 million, but $750 million is probably a better number – you may be able to start a family office and attract a competent, experienced, full-time chief investment officer. At minimum, family office investment teams have two to four professionals, but they may have a dozen or more. Attracting and retaining people who are experienced at creating value is expensive, but likely to pay for itself multiple times over. In contrast, an underfunded personnel budget, or a hiring strategy based on loyalty rather than competence, runs the risk of being penny wise and pound foolish. You will also need team members for record keeping, tax, and administrative support. This team needs to be managed; it's a big governance commitment. If you have financial assets between $25 million and $500 million, the price points of an adequately resourced single-family investment office strongly suggest an outsourced solution.

If you have a complex estate and work with an outsourced advisor, I encourage you to seek one with four essential characteristics. First, they should develop a comprehensive understanding of your family and financial objectives, relevant contours of your family tree, and the structure of your wealth. Second, that comprehensive perspective should inform a disciplined, interdisciplinary, and integrative approach to managing wealth, one that measures, however imperfectly, the multiple ways to add value to your family's well-being as well as to your assets. Third, the advisor should be a fiduciary, acting purely on your behalf and putting your interests ahead of his or her own.

Before moving to point four, we should explore some nuances of being a fiduciary. From a regulatory perspective, an institutional trustee or an independent Registered Investment Advisor (RIA) are the simplest, cleanest fits as trusted, comprehensive, strategic advisors. They clearly meet the third standard listed above: they are fiduciaries. Broker-dealer firms and "private banks" may also have affiliates that act with full fiduciary responsibility. But you are stepping into a gray area. These institutions provide essential financial services that RIAs cannot, including deposit accounts, lending, securities trading, and the creation of derivate securities. Simplistically, they have the capacity to "rent" their balance sheets to their clients as part of their services. Independent RIAs don't. However, these full-service institutions also have a more complex task managing conflicts of interest; the broker-dealer "suitability" standard of care that applies to these institutions is a lower standard of client care than the RIA fiduciary duty.

Use your fiduciary in that personal trainer capacity to help you become a more informed buyer of brokerage, banking, or insurance services. If you choose a broker-dealer or private bank as your strategic advisor, you must remain aware that they are not always required to act in your best interest. In any case, if the advisor or their firm receives third-party compensation for making recommendations to you, or you have to buy their products in order to access their advice, you will never know whether their financial incentives are aligned with yours. Be sure to clarify these points and codify them in your advisory contract and/or in your IPS.

Numerous advisory firms build their value propositions around these first three criteria: a comprehensive perspective, interdisciplinary process, and a fiduciary mindset. But their cultures and histories are often steeped in active management of investments. This is where delivery of their value proposition can unravel. As I explained in Chapter 8, it makes no sense to promote actively managed taxable portfolios that closely track their benchmark, yet this is often what is on offer. As you've seen, for such portfolios, tax drag almost always overwhelms any positive value added from investment decisions.

If your portfolio does not track the index because it has high tracking error, at least you have a chance to succeed, but the cost of making wrong decisions is also higher. Clients like to beat the market. But trying to do so through high-tracking-error managers is risky; at points along the path to outperformance, they inevitably underperform, sometimes by a lot and sometimes for several years. That underperformance may cause a client to become impatient with the manager at the wrong time, and possibly with their advisor, too. It's an investment risk and a business risk that some advisors prefer to avoid.

That's why the fourth essential characteristic you need is an advisor sufficiently dedicated to you and your objectives, whom you trust and respect to help guide you through challenging times.

If a portion of your portfolio is actively managed, he or she must be skilled at researching and selecting superior active managers (or be closely surrounded by those who are). He or she should also have a nuanced understanding of your portfolio, your tax position, and the estate planning structures through which you invest.

Clients look to their advisors to access managers that can outperform. Over the years, I've often asked myself two questions: "What investment styles and manager characteristics are most likely to deliver the long-term results clients seek?" and "How can our firm's expensive research talent be allocated efficiently to identify the managers with those qualifying characteristics?"

Here is how I have addressed these questions over the last 20-plus years on behalf of my family and our firm's other clients. First, eliminate high turnover and low-tracking-error managers in public equity markets, especially ones with above average fees. Second, focus on less efficient and less liquid parts of the financial markets where the odds of success are higher. Third, focus on tax-efficient investments; this eliminates most fixed income and hedge funds. These three simple steps substantially reduce the number of investment options to be evaluated and eliminate most managers with the biggest gap between headline performance and the net dollars that end up in taxable client pockets. Following this approach, I've no doubt missed a handful of potentially great opportunities, but I've been able to allocate costly research resources where they are most likely to make a difference to client performance. In high-tracking-error investing, each decision is important and deserves full expert attention. Making targeted and well-informed investment decisions is wiser than spreading yourself thin to cover the waterfront.

Fourth, with the right talent appropriately focused, develop conviction to make few enough and large enough investments that each can make a positive difference to overall results. As a practical matter, it should take years to build a mature portfolio of actively managed assets in less efficient markets. I wouldn't expose more than 10% to 15% of my portfolio to any single "vintage year." As a general rule, a specialized, high-return potential private fund investment should be no less than a 1% commitment; otherwise it's too small to move the needle. On the other hand, I would not commit more than 3% to 4% of assets to a single private investment fund, even if it is broadly diversified. There is just too much beyond my control that can go wrong. Following my recommended approach, over multiple vintages, through a combination of net cash flow and appreciation, clients can grow a series of material commitments with a single active manager into a 7%, 8%, even 10% position. Above 10%, especially when the investment is illiquid, the specific organizational risk of the manager would give me pause.

Fifth, proactively seek opportunity; don't wait for it to come to you. I once had a boss – and brilliant investor – who regularly asked people selling him investment ideas, "If this is such a great investment, why are you showing it to me instead of doing it yourself?" Average investments are common and easily found. Really good investments are scarce and valuable opportunities.

Sixth, we ask whether our insights, our network, our capital, or our managers' insights and infrastructure are differentiated in a way that should lead to superior results. It's easy for us to fool ourselves into believing we have differentiated skill and insight, though we try not to. Managers' marketing materials are designed to convince you that they have that special sauce that leads, time and again, to superior results.

My approach requires a lot of shoe leather. It requires saying "no" quickly and most of the time, and "yes" slowly. It also mandates a single-minded focus on serving clients. Selecting investment ideas on the basis of whether that manager will pay a distribution fee or based on how much money you can deploy in a strategy may be good business decisions but that is different than making good investment decisions. My clients care only about the latter.

Comprehensive information is key to monitoring the effectiveness of a manager selection process at both the firm level and client by client. Unless you're really unskilled or unlucky, selecting a series of high-tracking-error managers almost guarantees that some will succeed handsomely. The successes offer bragging rights and scintillating cocktail conversation. They are the fodder that creates the aura of success without in any way assuring actual success – if success is defined as aggregate investment value added. Without a good system of accountability for your total portfolio, it's easy to fool yourself into believing that your strategy is working.

Likewise, a portfolio of high-tracking-error investment managers also means that some will fail to meet expectations, sometimes by a lot. Even the best manager identification process makes mistakes. The higher the tracking error, the greater the potential impact of those errors. Broadly, there are two types of failures. There are the more obvious failures: those managers whose investments decline in value and don't recover. The insidious failures are those that underperform for long periods but still show a profit. They represent opportunity cost relative to just investing simply and inexpensively in an index. Make sure your measurement system captures the combined effects of all your investment decisions, as well as the impact of each decision. Otherwise you can keep fooling yourself for a long time. I say this to financial advisors as well as to the clients they serve.

If you want to generate superior long-term, after-tax performance, finding the right advisor demands that you ask tough questions. Does the advisor think and act like a principal? Is their active manager research team well-trained, experienced, focused, and accountable for delivering superior performance to the firm's clients? Does the firm think, act, and measure at the intersection of investment, tax, and estate planning? Can they guide you to other financial service providers as needed, and coordinate their delivery? Do they have the systems and discipline to get the myriad little things right? Do they manage their own wealth with the same philosophy and the same tools that they manage yours? Do they derive their fee income solely from service to you, or do they also have fee arrangements with vendors of various sorts? Are they fiduciaries and do they act accordingly?

That advisor, whether an individual or a team, whether outsourced or full-time, will not be easy to find. When you think you have one, you'll need to dig deep. Try to ascertain whether there is alignment between your goals as the client and the advisor's attributes. How does their marketing pitch line up with their abilities, incentives, access to qualified resources, and the means to measure your results and their value added?

For a wealth advisory firm, it is challenging to provide an integrated service, especially one that is customized to each client's personal circumstances and objectives, and without conflicts of interest. Whether clients are looking for a simple solution or a complex one, to achieve optimal results and to obtain the quality of service I describe, clients should want to pay their chosen advisor reasonably well. Why? The firm should be profitable enough to thrive for decades to come. It needs to attract, retain, and compensate talented, ethical people who see wealth management as a calling, not just a job. It needs people who can work across multiple disciplines in depth, not superficially. It needs access to expensive investment, legal, and tax experts. Each client's portfolio contains a lot of complexity, often fragmented into multiple legal and tax structures, and hundreds or thousands of tax lots that need to be managed day to day and then consolidated to view the whole picture. To complicate matters further, one "client" may include multiple family members, each with several portfolios and different objectives, estate plans, and communication styles, not to mention calendars. To manage all that takes experience, talent, coordination, and access to robust and secure systems, whether internal or outsourced. Working with a taxable client family is a much bigger job than advising a typical pension plan or endowment of similar size.

Once an integrated, long-term strategy is codified into an investment policy, the value created by a skilled interdisciplinary team comes in lots of small incremental decisions, over decades. It's the same with your personal trainer. You and your advisor must manage regularly and consistently, sometimes for years, methodically building value and remaining vigilant. Cross-disciplinary training, regular and keen attention to detail, and comprehensive understanding of your circumstances are central tenets to success, enabling you, in partnership with the right advisor, to catalyze the trajectory of your wealth and of your legacy. From time to time, you will also experience major transitions that impact your financial circumstances. You may sell a business or liquidate a big stock position. You may retire. A recession may spring open estate planning opportunities. You may receive an inheritance. How you and your advisory team handle these major transitions can create or destroy enormous value. Prepare for them in advance if possible and work with trusted folks who have been through them before. Harkening back to the first few paragraphs of this book, the right strategy plus effective teamwork can be worth millions of dollars to you and bring your family financial peace of mind.

KEY CHAPTER TAKEAWAYS

- Think of your financial advisor as a personal trainer to help manage your wealth.
- Managing taxable wealth can be simple and indexed or complicated and actively managed. You need to choose the right path for you, and then select the right advisor.
- With a simple approach, most people – alone or in partnership with their advisor – can invest successfully in broadly diversified target date funds, index funds, and ETFs.
- If you go the more complex, active management route, select one advisor with four essential characteristics: 1) a comprehensive understanding of your family and financial objectives, 2) an interdisciplinary and integrative approach to managing wealth, 3) a legal and cultural fiduciary responsibility to act on their clients' behalf, and 4) an investment research system designed and measured to optimize after-tax performance.
- Seek value at the intersection of investing, cash flow management, tax, and estate planning.
- Make sure your advisor is sufficiently compensated to attract and retain a qualified team.
- The combination of the right wealth management strategy and the right advisor can be worth millions of dollars to you and bring your family financial peace of mind.

APPENDIX

Additional Books about Taxable Investing

Bernstein, William J. *The Four Pillars of Investing: Lessons for Building a Winning Portfolio.* McGraw Hill, 2010.

Ellis, Charles D. *Winning the Loser's Game: Timeless Strategies for Successful Investing,* especially Chapter 14, "The Individual Investor." McGraw Hill, 2002.

Evensky, Harold, Stephen M. Horan, and Thomas R. Robinson. *The New Wealth Management: The Financial Advisor's Guide to Managing and Investing Client Assets.* John Wiley & Sons, 2011.

Gallati, Reto R. *Tax-Efficient Investing: Strategies for Maximizing Your Investment Income.* CreateSpace Independent Publishing Platform, 2013.

Gannon, Niall J. *Investing Strategies for the High Net Worth Investor: Maximize Returns on Taxable Portfolios.* McGraw Hill Education, 2010.

Gordon, Robert N., with Jan M. Rosen. *Wall Street Secrets for Tax-Efficient Investing: From Tax Pain to Investment Gain.* Bloomberg Press, 2001

Larimore, Taylor, Mel Lindauer, and Michael LeBoeuf. *The Bogle-heads' Guide to Investing,* 2nd ed. John Wiley & Sons, 2014.

Lucas, Stuart E. *Wealth: Grow It and Protect It,* updated and revised. FT Press, 2012.

Rogers, Douglas S., CFA. *Tax-Aware Investment Management: The Essential Guide.* Bloomberg Press, 2006.

Siegel, Jeremy J. *Stocks for the Long Run: The Definitive Guide to Financial Market Returns and Long-Term Investment Strategies,* 5th ed. McGraw Hill Education, 2014.

Wilcox, Jarrod, Jeffrey E. Horvitz, and Dan DiBartolomeo. *Investment Management for Taxable Private Investors.* Research Foundation of CFA Institute, 2008.

Index